THE UNAUTHORIZED GUIDE TO DOING
BUSINESS THE
ALAN SUGAR
WAY

THE UNAUTHORIZED GUIDE TO DOING BUSINESS THE

ALAN SUGAR

WAY

10 SECRETS OF THE BOARDROOM'S TOUGHEST INTERVIEWER

By Emma Murray

CAPSTONE

Registered office
Capstone Publishing Ltd. (A Wiley Company), The Atrium, Southern Gate,
Chichester, West Sussex, PO19 8SQ, United Kingdom
For details of our global editorial offices, for customer services and for
information about how to apply for permission to reuse the copyright material
in this book please see our website at www.wiley.com.

Library of Congress Cataloguing-in-Publication Data is available

9781907312441

A catalogue record for this book is available from the British Library.

Set in Myriad Pro by Sparks (www.sparkspublishing.com)
Printed in Great Britain by TJ International Ltd, Padstow, Cornwall

CONTENTS

ACKNOWLEDGEMENTS

I'd like to think that this book is a fair interpretation of why Alan Sugar has been so successful over the last 40 years. Whether you view him as a belligerent bruiser or a savvy revolutionary of the technology industry, there is no denying that he is an intriguing character. For over four decades, he has made headlines as a business mogul, football chairman, government adviser and media phenomenon – and his star is in no danger of fading. These days, Sugar is best known as the straight-talking, no-nonsense, charismatic presenter of the reality TV show *The Apprentice*. However, there is much more to him than his natural presenting skills. His lifelong contribution to business, his commitment to helping others (especially young people) achieve their goals, and the donation of his free time and his money to charity deserve more than just a brief mention.

A great deal of research has been carried out in writing this book. In particular, I would recommend David Thomas's excellent book, *The Amstrad Story*, Charlie Burden's *Sir Alan Sugar: The Biography*, and, of course, Alan Sugar's very informative *The Apprentice: How To Get Hired Not Fired*. A special mention also goes to the show itself, *The Apprentice* on BBC, which has also been a source of inspiration.

I would also like to thank Emma Swaisland at Wiley-Capstone for providing me with the opportunity to write about such a fascinating character. Finally, heartfelt thanks to Sam – for keeping the faith.

THE LIFE AND TIMES OF ALAN SUGAR

As the most talked about entrepreneur in Britain, Alan Sugar is well on his way to achieving legendary status. Throughout his impressive career, Sugar has worn many hats: business entrepreneur, property mogul, airline founder, football club chairman, generous benefactor, charitable donator, media star … the list goes on. Not forgetting, of course, his knighthood in 2000 and his peerage in 2009.

However, there is one title that Sugar deserves as much, if not more, as the others: World's Toughest Negotiator. As early as his teens, Sugar was negotiating deals that would make a man twice his age gasp in admiration. Later on, he demonstrated his nerves of steel by taking on the big boys like IBM, and the large corporations in the City. A natural negotiator, Sugar is fearless when it comes to making a deal. His Amstrad days may be over, but his negotiating skills still play an important part in his own business interests; whether he is securing a deal to build up his impressive property portfolio for Amsprop, coming up with creative ideas for Amscreen, the digital signage company, or working out a strategy to suit his private aircraft charter company, Amsair.

Richard Branson operates in business with a smile on his face that belies his ruthless negotiating skills, while behind Sugar's gruffness is a genuine warmth and sense of humour that proves attractive to the prospective client. Getting the balance right between Mr Nice Guy and Mr Tough-As-Old-Boots is a difficult one, but Sugar pulls it off with a certain degree of finesse, and is, in fact, far nicer and less scary than he appears.

Nicknamed 'Mopsy' as a child because of his cloud of dark, curly hair, the working class boy from east London grew up to conquer not only the business world but society in general. As the demanding, straight-talking and brutally honest presenter of *The Appren-*

tice, Sugar has both amused and scared us from our screens, but he admits that he is a lot less scary in real life. Love him or loathe him, there is no doubt that Sugar is fast becoming a National Treasure, although he would probably never admit it.

There is no denying that this is a man that has made a huge impression on not only the business world but also on people across a wide demographic, and achieved a tremendous amount of success over a relatively short period of time. Call him whatever name you wish – Sir Alan Sugar, Lord Sugar, Baron Sugar … but call him 'Mopsy' at your peril.

THE PRECOCIOUS CHILD

Alan Michael Sugar was born in Hackney, east London, to Nathan and Fay Sugar in March 1947. He was the youngest of four with an eleven-year gap between him and the nearest siblings, the twins, Derek and Daphne. His mother recalled that, right from the beginning, he was a bossy and noisy baby, which doesn't seem surprising given his character.

However, despite early signs of obstreperousness, Sugar was a rather quiet child who kept himself to himself and maintained a distance from the other children who played among the blocks of flats that made up the Northwold estate where he lived. It appeared that from a very young age, childish games were not for him, and he preferred to spend his time alone.

Money was always short in the Sugar household. Nathan Sugar was a struggling tailor who worked in the garment trade. Jobs were not easy to come by in post-war Britain and Nathan often spent weeks looking for work.

Alan Sugar learned from an early age that if he wanted pocket money, he would have to get it himself. As a small child, he would go around the flats, knocking on neighbours' doors asking if he could collect their empty pop bottles. He would then return his quarry to the shop, receiving a few pennies in return. In his early teens, he was given a gift of a ginger beer plant. He learned how to make ginger beer out of it, bottled the contents, and sold it to his classmates at school. This was Sugar's first experience of manufacturing; already he had come up with a business formula that worked time and again within the company he would later found: look for a product that was in demand; produce that product cheaply; undercut competitors (Coca-Cola was far more expensive for his schoolmates to buy than his homemade ginger beer); and sell the cheaper product to those that could not afford the brands.

But his extra-curricular activities didn't stop there. The teenage Alan Sugar boiled raw beetroot for the local greengrocer, helped out on a market stall, took photos of neighbours and their children and sold them to the families, sold photographic films that he cut into camera-sized rolls to schoolmates, and worked in a department store selling shoes.

Although he was showing promise as an entrepreneur and businessman, Sugar was underwhelmed by school and academic learning. He failed his 11+ exam and attended a technical secondary school where he was most interested in metalwork and technical drawing. He also had an interest in science that would be put to good use later on in his business. A distinctly average student, Sugar stayed in school long enough to earn himself a few O-levels and left his academic life for good at the age of 16. By that time, he was making more money than his father from his various sidelines.

The young Alan Sugar was very much influenced by his father's fruitless efforts to earn money for the family, and decided very early on that he would never follow in his father's footsteps: 'I didn't want to have to live that way. While I was at school, I was making more money, selling bits and pieces, than my father was earning.'[1]

THE WHEELER-DEALER

After he left school, Sugar spent a year in an ill-fated role in the Civil Service, working in the statistics department of the Ministry of Education and Science. Instantly bored by the 9 to 5 office job, Sugar left the Ministry, but ended up in another white-collar role. He soon realized that he got more of a kick out of his Saturday sidelines than he did in his uninspiring desk job, and decided to explore his entrepreneurial skills full-time.

A venture selling reconditioned televisions with a friend followed, before accepting a sales role with Robuk Electrical. The young Sugar had finally found his niche: sales was exactly the area he wanted to be in. He quickly excelled in his role but, in a way, was a victim of his own success. Although he made great deals for Robuk, he was stinted on his commission, and he walked away from that job.

A similar role at the electrical wholesaler Henson followed and it was during that time that Sugar really began to see the potential of setting up on his own. He bought a van and started to sell electrical goods to retailers. Being self-employed suited the restless Sugar but he soon realized that he would need to grow his business in order to make it a real success.

THE ENTREPRENEUR

In 1968, two life-changing events occurred for the 21-year-old Alan Sugar. He founded his own company called Amstrad, which was created out of the initials of his full name: **A**lan **M**ichael **S**ugar **Trad**ing; and he married his teenage sweetheart, Ann Simons. Sugar had first spotted his bride-to-be at the tender age of 17 and from the outset was determined to make her his.

At first, Simons' family were a little sceptical of the match, believing that the young hairdresser could do better, so Sugar set out to prove them wrong. He worked hard to build up his business and to prove to his future in-laws that he would be able to provide for their daughter. A few years later, they relented and Sugar and Simons were finally married, a union that continues to last 40 years on.

At first, Amstrad was strictly about buying and selling electrical goods, much of it imported. Sugar would import cigarette lighters and intercoms, and badge them: the first items to bear the Amstrad brand. Sugar spent the first couple of years of his new business making contacts with retailers and outlets with a view to selling his imported goods to them further down the line. He also invested in a retail store with a partner called Global Audio, which sold audio supplies, but soon opted out of the venture: he had bigger fish to fry.

By 1970, Sugar realized that a pure buying and selling operation had its limitations. He decided to take his business to a new level and so turned his attention to the hi-fi market. At the time, the parts that made up the hi-fi were sold separately and each part was sold at quite a high price. Through research, Sugar realized he could manufacture at least one part cheaply: the plastic covers that were used to keep the dust off the turntable. By investing in an injection-moulding tool, he was soon making dust covers more cheaply than any of his competitors. By keeping his prices low, margins large and volumes high, the product was an instant hit with wholesalers, retailers and, in particular, customers. Amstrad's first foray into manufacturing was a resounding success.

Amstrad soon began to manufacture a range of all sorts of electronic goods: amplifiers, an all-in-one hi-fi called the Tower System, tuners, tape decks and speakers all hit the market to huge success. For the first time, a company was designing products for the mass market, and retailers and consumers alike couldn't get enough of them. Huge retailers like Comet, Rumbelows, Currys and Woolworths were clamouring to do business with the young entrepreneur, and he soon had a range of suppliers all over the world to meet the demand.

However, the Amstrad fan club did not just consist of consumers and retailers – top executives in the City were beginning to sit up and take notice. There were murmurings about Sugar's golden touch and his talent for bringing innovative products to market. The Amstrad effect, as it soon became known, had taken over the electronic market, and the financiers knew that Sugar was a man who was going places. Baffled at first by this plain-speaking, scruffy-looking young man, the stockbrokers soon saw the potential in Sugar and his company's meteoric rise to success. They were proved right. When Amstrad was floated on the London Stock Exchange in 1980, it doubled its profits each year during the early 1980s.

Although Sugar was becoming one of the wealthiest men in Britain, he didn't see this as a reason to rest on his laurels. Ignoring all warnings from his City advisers, he decided to enter the home computer market. Again, Amstrad's philosophy was applied to this new product: find a way to manufacture them cheaply, sell at a lower price thus undercutting competitors, and target the mass market. Once more, Sugar had chosen a winning product and successfully managed to steer his company in an entirely new direction. More computer models were produced, followed by the first mass-market dedicated word processor. At its peak, Amstrad was worth a staggering £1.2 billion, and its founder was named the fifteenth richest man in Britain in 1989.

However, by the late 1980s, Amstrad's star was beginning to wane. The 1987 stock market crash, the rising price of computer components, labour shortages and faulty products all contributed to Amstrad's financial losses. Sugar admits that Amstrad expanded too fast to meet the growing demand and had started to make mistakes from which it would never recover. During the 1990s Amstrad had some success with some of its products, but not on the same scale as before. However, a lucrative deal with Sky to manufacture satellite receivers put Amstrad firmly back on the map.

In 2007, Alan Sugar sold his life's work to BSkyB and stepped down as Chairman and CEO of Amstrad, fully resigning in July 2009. However, his business career is far from over. Sugar keeps himself occupied with investing in property, and two other companies run by his sons, Daniel and Simon.

THE FOOTBALL CHAIRMAN

In 1991, Sugar, as unpredictable as ever, took a surprising interest in the football club Tottenham Hotspur. For 10 years he used his position as chairman to save the club from financial ruin. However, it was not an easy time for the businessman, who fell out of favour with Tottenham fans for firing their beloved former player and manager, Terry Venables. Sugar battled through court cases, physical attacks and threats from fans, and a media onslaught so vicious that it would furnish a life-long suspicion of journalists.

Although his decade at Tottenham was one of the bleakest periods of his life, he stuck it out, determined to finish what he started – and thanks to him, the club is still thriving today.

THE POLITICAL ACTIVIST

Hailed by many as Thatcher's darling, Sugar was a shining light in the business world and proved that someone who came from nothing could make it with a good dose of common sense, hard work, grit and determination.

Sugar didn't just break through class barriers – he shattered them and, in doing so, inspired young people all over the country to follow his example. Although a keen admirer of the Iron Lady, Sugar believed that the Conservative Party lost their way after the departure of their leader, and later chose to support Labour, to which he has donated generously.

A staunch patriot, Sugar has remained one of the Labour party's most loyal supporters and has taken part in many campaigns and government schemes set up to help small businesses and graduates, and to inspire youth enterprise. Sugar's involvement with the British government reached new heights in 2000 when he received a knighthood for services to business and for his charity work. In 2009, he was offered a peerage and made an official adviser to the government to share his business expertise and help struggling businesses.

The boy from Hackney now goes by three rather grand-sounding titles: Sir Alan Sugar (by which he is most popularly known), Lord Sugar and Baron Sugar of Clapton, in the London Borough of Hackney.

THE MEDIA STAR

These days, Alan Sugar is best known for his down-to-earth nature and cutting wit as hard-hitting boss 'Sir Alan' in *The Apprentice*. Over the course of 12 weeks, Sugar puts 14 applicants through their paces in order to find his next apprentice. Each week, the candidates must work within their teams to win the assigned task. The losing team must face the wrath of Sugar in the boardroom, who ends up firing one or more of them, usually for incompetence, carelessness, unprofessionalism, poor leadership abilities and a general lack of the qualities he expects from his employees. The process continues until only the strongest are left standing, and the battle is on to see who will become Sugar's next apprentice. Many of the winning apprentices from the show are still working in one of Sugar's various businesses today.

There is no play-acting where Alan Sugar is concerned; what you see is what you get, and he can't abide people who try and imitate his style or attempt to mirror his body language in order to ingratiate themselves to him. He prefers people who 'get to the point as quickly as possible, are logical, honest and straightforward.'[2] That is the real Alan Sugar; he may be gruff but he is always honest and straight down the line, so it is not surprising that he values those same qualities in others.

It is clear that Sugar's ability to stay true to himself has not only gained the respect and admiration from his peers in the business world, but has successfully won over a sizeable audience as a TV personality. A record eight million viewers tuned into the launch of the fifth series of *The Apprentice,* aired in March 2009 – the highest ratings yet. Thus, it seems like Sugar is growing in popularity year upon year.

Even high-profile celebrities are getting in on the act. *Comic Relief Does The Apprentice* has proved highly successful, with well-known figures like Jonathan Ross, Cheryl Cole and Piers Morgan lining up to win the approval of the no-nonsense entrepreneur. Not only has the special version of the show attracted an even larger following, but it has raised a substantial amount for Comic Relief.

A sophisticated reality show, *The Apprentice* is educational as well as sensational. There is no other show on television that provides such an entertaining insight into the way business is conducted, or teaches people how to behave in a professional manner. It has met with huge success since it was launched in 2004, and Sugar has attracted a massive following as a result. It is clear that his no-non-sense, common-sense approach appeals to a wide demographic, and he has grown even more popular than ever with both young and old over the last few years.

KEY ACHIEVEMENTS

- **1970–1980:** Major success with first foray into manufacturing. Amstrad severely undercuts competitors by manufacturing low cost hi-fi turntable covers by using an injection-moulding machine rather than the more expensive vacuuming method. Products such as audio amplifiers and tuners soon follow, with similar success.

- **1980–1990:** Amstrad is listed on the London Stock Exchange and doubles in size every year during the early part of the 1980s. Amstrad launches the first affordable Home Computer for the mass market, followed by a Word Processor. In 1989, Sky TV commissions Amstrad to manufacture a satellite receiver/dish package in a highly lucrative deal. Amstrad also launches a new product: a combined fax, telephone and answering machine, which captures 52% of the personal fax market.

- **1990–2000:** On behalf of Sky TV, Amstrad launches the first integrated satellite receiver/decoder. Amstrad purchases shares in Betacom, a UK-based domestic telephone supplier, and acquires the Danish telecommunications manufacturer Dancall Telecom for £6.4 million. In 1997, Amstrad sells Dancall Telecom to Bosch for £95 million. Amstrad also acquires Viglen Technology, one of Britain's largest manufacturers of personal computers. When Viglen is floated separately on the London Stock Exchange in 1997, it returns some £200 million to Amstrad shareholders.

- **2000–present:** Amstrad launches the e-m@iler, a combined telephone, internet and emailing device, followed two years later with the e-m@ilerplus. Amstrad signs more deals with BSkyB to manufacture set-top boxes and agrees to supply a high definition (HD) set-top box for Sky Italia. In 2007, BSkyB acquires Amstrad, which is then delisted from the London Stock Exchange. A year later, Sugar steps down as Chairman and CEO of Amstrad, and resigns from Amstrad in July 2009.

CURRENT BUSINESS INTERESTS

It is a popular belief that Sugar spends most of his time pointing at the quivering *Apprentice* candidates, and uttering his immortal catchphrase, 'You're fired'. However, outside his role as media presenter, he has a number of other interests. He is the owner of Amsprop, an investment company that develops and owns property all over the UK. Recently, Amsprop branched out to secure a lucrative deal in Spain, where Sugar snapped up a £35 million five-star hotel for the bargain price of just £2.5 million. Other business interests include Amscreen, a digital advertising company, and Amsair Executive Aviation, which offers business and executive jet charters.

CHARITY WORK

Deservedly proud of his charitable activities, Alan Sugar willingly gives his own free time to support government schemes and tours the country to make public appearances and give speeches. He is

also a patron of the Hackney Empire theatre and generous benefactor of Great Ormond Street children's hospital. The Alan Sugar
Foundation was set up in 1986 and continues to donate to charitable concerns.

HOBBIES

A true advocate of working hard and playing hard, Sugar has a
number of pursuits in which he likes to engage during his time
off. He is a keen pilot and owner of a four-seat Cirrus SR20 aircraft.
He also enjoys collecting classic Rolls-Royce and Bentley motor-
cars. A fitness fanatic, he plays tennis regularly, and thinks nothing
of cycling 50 miles through the Essex countryside at least twice a
week. When he is not flying his plane or chalking up the miles on
his bike, he can be found relaxing at his luxurious holiday homes
in Spain and Florida.

1

DON'T PUSH OR SHOVE

'What you see on screen is me, there's no question of that … It's a one-way portrayal, not the whole of me.' [1]

– Alan Sugar

As the hard-nosed taskmaster on *The Apprentice* Alan Sugar has a reputation for being gruff, tough and notoriously intolerant of fools. His no-nonsense approach has earned him admiration from his legions of followers, but also criticism from several quarters. It appears that Sugar's style has the capacity to divide public opinion: there are those that love him for his forthrightness and ability to tell it like it is, versus others who feel his tough-talking approach falls into bullying territory. Then there are those who just find him plain scary.

Indeed, in a 2007 *Radio Times* poll consisting of 5000 people, Sugar was ranked seventh out of the Top 10 scariest TV celebrities in the UK, with Gordon Ramsay leading the pack. Although most viewers are aware that many of Sugar's reprimands are meted out with a firm twinkle in his eye, his management style has caused controversy among other groups, some of whom have branded him a bully.

The late Sir John Harvey-Jones, former chairman of ICI and presenter of business shows such as *Troubleshooter*, spoke out publicly against Sugar's fondness for plain-speaking. In an interview with *Management Today* in 2006, Harvey-Jones stated: 'I watch his programme with horror. If I had behaved that way for one day at ICI, I'd have been hot-stuffed and rightly.'[2]

Similarly, the charity Kidscape, set up to protect children from bullying and sexual abuse, believe that *The Apprentice* 'contributes to the problem of bullying'. However, Sugar, himself, has also voiced his concerns about how he has been portrayed in *The Apprentice*:

'It's frustrating for people who really know me – friends and family – who know I'm not really like that. To keep a team of loyal staff like I have for 30 years you can't go around being a bully.' [3]

Surely Sugar has a point. Bullies alienate people; they don't tend to attract a loyal following or feel motivated enough to provide help and support to others. Sugar did not build up his business empire all by himself, but created a vast network of advisers and friends, and has a list of business contacts that would make the eyes of any aspiring entrepreneur water. It is doubtful that so many people would have stood by him all these years if he was considered a bully, and he certainly would not have been chosen as a role model for youth enterprise by the government.

There is a major difference between bullying and assertiveness, and Sugar has the latter in spades.

It is true that Sugar has a unique personality and unconventional business style that has come into conflict, more than once, with the more conservative City business types – who in the past have been quite vocal in their suspicions about the level of Sugar's business acumen. However, his sharp business mind and uncanny ability to make good decisions has won the respect of his contemporaries (albeit sometimes grudgingly).

But just because he doesn't pull any punches when it comes to his communication style, doesn't mean he throws any, either. There is a major difference between bullying and assertiveness, and Sugar has the latter in spades.

SPEAK YOUR MIND

'I try to leave out the parts that people skip.'

Elmore Leonard

In a world where some might say business jargon has gone completely out of control, Sugar's direct style is definitely refreshing. His jargon-free approach has proved extremely popular to hundreds of thousands of viewers, and won the admiration of many top-level business executives who not only envy Sugar's management style but the fact that he can get away with it, without fear of reprisal. Never one for couching his language in bland or difficult-to-understand phrases, Sugar's work colleagues, employees and apprentices always know where they stand.

Sugar has always been an advocate of plain speaking and believes that communication should be clear, concise and well-defined, something that also extends to the written word. An anecdote from his Amstrad days illustrates Sugar's impatience for unclear communication: when he read the complex instruction manual that was to accompany the new Amstrad computer, to be launched in 1985, the language that had been used outraged him. The manual was full of complicated jargon that Sugar knew his target audience would simply not understand. So he demanded they create a simpler version in more relatable language, as he knew that the complex manual would alienate a large proportion of his intended target market.

Language full of pretentious business jargon is misleading, confusing and can leave a new employee completely mystified. Using jargon is often a smoke and mirrors exercise intended to bewitch the audience into believing that the speaker knows what he is talking about (even when he has no idea himself).

When filing out of a meeting following a particularly harrowing jargon-stuffed session, it is not uncommon for a new employee to feel 'out of the loop' and completely baffled as to the nature of the 'actionables' imposed in the meeting. In fact, in the cut-throat world of business where being quick on the uptake is an absolute prerequisite, in some organizations, an unfamiliarity with corporate-speak can really hinder a career. One business analyst remembers his first few weeks in his new job at an investment bank and the confusion he experienced after every meeting:

> *'When I first joined an investment bank, I used to go into meetings and come out none the wiser as to what exactly took place. I didn't know any of the business jargon, and when I looked at my notes they made no sense at all. I just knew it was fundamentally important to think "outside the box", but I had no idea what that meant. I am attracted to Sir Alan's jargon-free approach as it is refreshing and cathartic. Cathartic, meaning that it is a relief to see a manager speaking like a human being rather than a badly-programmed automaton.'*

Indeed, 'thinking outside the box', 'singing from the same hymn sheet', 'touching base' and 'blue sky thinking' are all phrases that have made it into the top ten most hated business phrases according to a survey carried out by the Internet Advertising Bureau in the UK (IAB UK). Even more dangerously, business jargon alienates people. A prospective client from outside the industry who is unfamiliar with the business buzzwords is more likely go in the opposite direction, and seek out the services of someone else that understands the value of plain speaking.

Alan Sugar has made a career out of speaking his mind. He admits that his abrupt manner has got him into hot water at times, but all in all, his honesty and directness has worked for rather than against him – and staying true to himself has won him a whole host of admirers over the years.

HAVE A TWINKLE IN YOUR EYE

Every business or corporation has its own work culture, designed to get the best out of their employees. Amstrad was built around Sugar's unique personality and direct approach, which obviously appealed to his legion of loyal supporters, many of whom worked for him for over 30 years. So why did they stick around for so long? Because behind his impatience and bluster is a very keen sense of humour that attracts people to the outwardly gruff business mogul.

Although Sugar may come across as somewhat crotchety in *The Apprentice*'s boardroom, it is important to note that he delivers criticism with a very bright twinkle in his eye. Far from being a one-dimensional character, Sugar has a great sense of humour that often has the viewers at home in stitches, and the apprentices themselves trying valiantly not to crack a smile.

It is not his brusque style that has made him a star, but his refreshing honesty, sincerity and humour. There are many TV personalities that have made a name for themselves through their honest, direct approach. Famously branded a bully by Hollie Steel, the 10-year-old former *Britain's Got Talent* contestant, Simon Cowell is the most obvious bad boy of television, with his acerbic wit and ability to reduce his *X Factor* and *Britain's Got Talent* hopefuls into pools of tears, but some would argue that he is in danger of becoming a caricature of himself. Gordon Ramsay is fond of cursing and doesn't make any allowances for his trembling protégés. Similarly, Peter Jones from *Dragon's Den* has become a little harsher on aspiring entrepreneurs over the last few years, but cannot quite seem to pull off his new direct stance.

However, Sugar manages to articulate in a style that is sensible, logical and constructive, relaying each message with a splash of humour and buckets of wit. Far from reducing his apprentices to tears, he manages to instil in them a sense of understanding, explaining exactly where they are going wrong and how they can learn from their mistakes. This is a management style that is almost impossible to emulate and it takes a certain type of personality to pull it off. Sugar sums it up well when he says to his apprentices, 'Don't start telling me that you're just like me, because no-one's like me; I'm unique.'

Sugar has always been an advocate of plain speaking and believes that communication should be clear, concise and well-defined.

ASSERTIVENESS RULES!

There is a vast difference between aggressive and bullying behaviour, and being assertive. Indeed, assertive communication is the most effective approach when we are dealing with others in a business environment. Poor communication, whether passive or aggressive, can cause divisions within teams and tension in relationships. Being assertive requires confidence and a healthy respect for others; it is about taking charge and getting the message across in a clear and defined manner, so that nobody is left in any doubt as to where they stand or the action they need to take.

Assertiveness comes from years of experience and being suffi-ciently self-aware to know how to communicate to others in such a way that the job gets done as quickly and as smoothly as pos-sible. It is a real skill to master assertiveness without coming across as aggressive or offensive. Many people in the work-place fear that if they try to be assertive, they will end up crossing the line into aggression.

Alan Sugar has made a career out of speaking his mind.

It is clear that Alan Sugar is a man who gets things done, and his management style is very much based on his skills as an assertive communicator. He makes no pretence about his firm approach, and it is his honesty and strength of character that has won him countless business deals over the last few dec-ades. From experience, he knows that asking direct questions, using plain and simple language, will generate the answers he wants.

Dr Michael Sinclair is a Consultant Psychologist and Managing and Clinical Director of City Psychology Group (CPG) based in the City of London, and regularly treats business executives. Dr Sinclair believes that:

> 'Assertive people are very popular and attractive to be around because they exude an air of certainty. Despite the fact that they may not tell us exactly what we want to hear, we always know where we stand with them. Assertive people lay down boundaries and set limits which gives us a sense of reassurance and stability, because we know how far we can push them – and when to stop. Sir Alan Sugar

is a typical example of an assertive person. He is confident, self-assured, focused and driven towards success, as well as being a clear communicator, a good speaker and a good listener.'

Tim Campbell, winner of the very first series of *The Apprentice*, also valued Alan Sugar's assertive approach: 'I come from a world where everything is politically correct. Being in a situation where things are actually expressed was quite refreshing. It may seem brutal, but for me it was always fair.'[4]

Treating people fairly is key to Sugar's communication technique. He may tell is like it is but he does not set out to humiliate or denigrate others. His main aim is to get the message across so he can provide them with some constructive criticism that will help them learn from their mistakes and do better in the future.

Certainly, he is competitive and driven, and his assertiveness shines through whenever he wants to get the best out of people or when he is in the depths of negotiation.

Sugar also has an inclusive style which means that everybody is involved in the communication and is clear about what is happening, the reasons behind it, who will be responsible for actioning the event, and what the outcome will be. He is a great believer in personal contact and prefers to talk face to face rather than over the phone or by email. Alan Sugar may be considered tough, scary even, but he is fair and makes sure that loyalty and hard work are always rewarded.

GIVE BULLIES SHORT SHRIFT

Throughout *The Apprentice*, Sugar has always maintained a tough stance against bullying and argumentative behaviour amongst the contestants, particularly when they are carrying out tasks.

Even so, there has been the odd public backlash as a result of heated arguments between the contestants; for example, in Series 4 of *The Apprentice*, caustic former sales manager, Jenny Celerier, appeared to pick on the rather eccentric Lucinda Ledgerwood, almost reducing her to tears. However, Sugar was quick to put a stop to the arguing in the boardroom and made it very clear that he would not tolerate argumentative and bullying behaviour: 'I am sick and tired of listening to you. Arguing is not constructive. Instead of arguing you should be drumming up business.'

Treating people fairly is key to Sugar's communication technique. He may tell it like it is but he does not set out to humiliate or denigrate others.

Similarly, Sugar took action over the behaviour of self-confessed 'ruthless alpha female', Katie Hopkins, during Series 3. Hopkins appeared to continually pass judgement on her fellow contestants, proclaiming on the show that rival Kristina Grimes was 'too orange to be taken seriously' and that Adam Hosker was rather too fond of wine, stating, 'when your best friends are Mr. Pinot and Mr. Grigio, you want to watch it'.

Although Hopkins made it to the final three, Sugar claims he had no intention of making her his next apprentice, as he didn't believe she was in the show for the right reasons. In one of *The*

Apprentice's most memorable moments, Hopkins stepped down from the competition, citing her family as the main reason for resigning from the show. So although Hopkins escaped being officially fired, Sugar made it very clear that her barbed attitude would simply not be tolerated in the business world and he would have fired her if she hadn't stepped down: 'She was never ever, ever going to win. Never in a million years. It sounds contradictory and it takes someone with big balls to see through it, but she was there for all the wrong reasons.'[5]

Alan Sugar expressed his outrage at her behaviour on *The Apprentice: You're Fired*, the after show hosted by Adrian Chiles, by saying, 'There's no way I could see how anyone could employ someone like that. There's something very sad there.'

So it is clear that Alan Sugar is not a man that will put up with aggressive and offensive behaviour either in the business world, or within *The Apprentice* teams, and is not shy about setting them straight about it.

DON'T BE A FUDDY-DUDDY

Sugar's style and unique personality transcends generations. Although he is in his sixties he is able to reach a younger audience, as well as an older one – truly a unique gift. In fact, Sugar's influence has spread across three generations: the Alan Sugar of the Amstrad years, his time at Tottenham Hotspur, and now *The Apprentice* years. Clearly the show's producers at Talkback Thames also have faith in his ability to attract a more youthful audience when it was announced in 2009 that he would host a younger version of *The Apprentice*.

In *Junior Apprentice*, which is to be launched in 2010, Sugar will be putting ten ambitious teenagers aged 16 and 17 through their paces over a five-part series. The winner will receive prize money of £25,000, which will go towards setting them up in their chosen career.

Love him or hate him, it is clear that the boy from east London must be doing something right.

Sugar has long been a champion of the next generation and has given countless speeches at universities all over the country, inspiring young minds to make their mark in the business world. He has always attracted a younger following and has become increasingly popular with the teenage audience. In fact, The Youth of Today survey commissioned in 2009 by the Prince's Trust revealed that teenagers rated Alan Sugar among the world's greatest leaders, including Barack Obama, Martin Luther King and Nelson Mandela.

Sugar has as much belief in young people as they do in him, telling *The Guardian*, 'It is my long-held belief that we should be doing more to promote enterprise among young people, as the future of our economy relies on them.' As enterprise czar, Sugar is also fronting a government campaign called Apprenticeships Make Things Happen, designed to encourage businesses to award apprenticeships to young people.

TV broadcaster and former *Smash Hits* editor Emma Jones explains why Sugar appeals to the younger generation:

> *'Because he comes from nothing, he gives young people the ideal to aim for; he inspires people. He has created a*

level playing field where anyone can be successful. When you're young and idealistic, that kind of goal can be irresistible. He's an authority figure, sort of like the strictest kind of school-teacher who you might be a bit scared of but for whom you have total respect. Indeed, Apprentice contestants strive to win his respect and approval as much as the prize. When young people are starting out in the workplace, they need a mentor to guide them. Alan Sugar has become everybody's mentor. To be liked by him is a real mark of respect and a badge of honour. He is truly a champion of young people.'

For a man that was voted the most inspiring business figure in the UK by the business social networking site BT Tradespace, love him or hate him, it is clear that the boy from east London must be doing something right.

DON'T PUSH OR SHOVE

Alan Sugar may be famous for his gruff manner and no-nonsense attitude, but he is no bully. His assertiveness and honesty has won him many a business deal, and the admiration of millions of people, inside and outside the business world.

- **Speak your mind.** Sugar's jargon-free approach allows him to communicate clearly and concisely, and leaves his listeners in no doubt as to where they stand and what they must do next.
- **Have a twinkle in your eye.** For all his bluntness and self-confessed belligerence, Sugar puts his point across with wit, humour and charisma, which have helped him to seal many a business deal, and win the loyalty of his employees and clients.
- **Assertiveness rules!** Part of being assertive is staying true to yourself. Nobody can pretend to be assertive, it is a skill that takes years of experience to refine. Sugar is naturally assertive. He manages to get his message across, using plain and simple language, a technique that always gets him the right answers.
- **Give bullies short shrift.** Time and again, Sugar has reprimanded his apprentices for arguing and back-stabbing. He was particularly outraged by Katie Hopkins' behaviour towards her fellow contestants and made sure that she was aware of his disapproval.
- **Don't be a fuddy-duddy.** Sugar has a style and personality that transcends generations. Teens aspire to follow in his footsteps and adults admire his sharp mind and keen business sense. Sugar has not let his age slow him down and shows no sign of retiring any time soon.

2
START A REVOLUTION

'Some years ago, someone described what we do as "the Amstrad effect" … it means bringing out something new, something that changes the world, changes the face of business. That's what I strive to do.'[1]

– Alan Sugar

The greatest entrepreneurs are revolutionaries. They have the drive to bring ideas to fruition, and take great personal and financial risks to make their goals a reality. In doing so, they have managed to revolutionize the way we think, what we buy and how we view the world.

Some of the world's most influential business revolutionaries are right on our doorstep: Richard Branson has brought fun and colour to the masses and the business world with his Virgin brand; Jamie Oliver has catered to a wide demographic by introducing a simpler way of cooking; and business mogul Philip Green has become a powerful force by turning around the performance of high street retailers. In their own way, these entrepreneurs have gambled their reputation and their livelihoods in order to put their own stamp on society.

Alan Sugar is certainly in good company. Indeed, he has much in common with other entrepreneurs: a drive and passion to succeed, together with a keen intellect and excellent business instincts. He also had the confidence to question the norm, and a thirst for fairness. During his Amstrad days, his main mission was to democratize society – to make products available to everybody, not just the elite. In this he succeeded tenfold, although the odds were very much against him from the beginning.

Alan Sugar grew up in an environment where money was scarce, and cars and televisions were regarded as luxury items, conserved for the wealthy. However, his impoverished background by no means held him back and he pursued his business interests with energy and enthusiasm. Even as a young man, Sugar felt a need to provide cheaper, more affordable products, and spent almost a year selling on reconditioned televisions to working class families at a lower rate. However, after he set up Amstrad, he decided that he wanted to innovate even further and on a much larger scale. A social revolution had begun.

DO YOUR HOMEWORK

When Sugar decided that he wanted Amstrad to manufacture products, he carried out a lot of industry research and soon found out a potential way to make money out of the hi-fi world. The plastic covers that hi-fi enthusiasts had to buy to protect the turntable from dust were inordinately expensive – and the aspiring entrepreneur wanted to know why. He realized that manufacturers used Perspex to make the covers, which was quite a pricey material at the time. So the young businessman set out to see if he could make it any cheaper. After many phone calls and a lot of enquiries, he discovered that there was a way to churn out the covers at a lower cost through a process called injection moulding.

During his Amstrad days, his main mission was to democratize society – to make products available to everybody, not just the elite.

He invested in an injection-moulding machine and, despite a few hiccups at the beginning, Amstrad started to manufacture and sell the dust covers, followed by plinths. These were the first products to be manufactured by Amstrad and when they arrived at the retailers, they flew off the shelves. This was a formula that Amstrad was to follow time and again. Sugar may not have invented anything, but he knew how to enhance a product's potential in a way that would appeal to his target market.

INNOVATION IS EVERYTHING

It is rare these days for a product to be created completely from scratch. Usually, a new product has its roots in another version but it has simply been enhanced. For example, the iPod is an innovative product whose history lies in hi-fis, Walkmans, Discmans and ghettoblasters. Yet, although this is a well-known fact, iPods continue to fascinate as they are a sleeker, better model of the original clunky personal stereos.

Sugar didn't use focus groups or formally carry out any real market research.

Following the success of the dust covers, Sugar knew he could not afford to be complacent. He knew he would have to innovate fast with a new product before his competitors caught up with him. If the bigger manufactures cottoned on to his injection-moulding scheme, they would inevitably be able to do it for an even cheaper rate that would end up pricing the Amstrad products out of the market.

So he turned his attention to amplifiers. At the time, amplifiers were an extremely expensive part of a hi-fi – and, like all elements of the hi-fi, they had to be bought separately. Although the amplifiers weren't the most high-tech on the market, they were cheap and for the first time teenagers had access to these much-desired speakers and at an affordable price.

Sugar realized that most working class youngsters didn't mind if the sound was top-notch or not, and that they couldn't care less about all the bells and whistles that came with the more expensive versions. These kids just wanted to be able to play their music in their bedrooms at a price they could afford: 'The hi-fi manufacturers were hung up on producing Aston Martins or Rolls-Royces of sound, but Sugar understood that the era of mass consumption demanded a Mini.'[2]

At this stage, Sugar knew he had the winning formula:

1   Find an existing product.

2   Get rid of unnecessary components.

3   Make it better.

4   Achieve a profit for the company.

5   Provide the customer with value for money.

This is a theory he applied time and again, with outstanding results. But it was a philosophy that was not without its risks. A self-confessed gambler when it comes to taking chances on new products, Sugar has always been a big believer in taking risks. His father Nathan believed in a steady job for life – perhaps growing up in that environment encouraged Sugar to rebel against the 'safe life' and take some chances. However, the young entrepreneur was never careless when it came to making decisions; his risks were calculated ones, based on market research and his own instincts for what the customer wanted.

So, once more, he turned his attention to the hi-fi market, but this time he looked at the bigger picture. It bothered him that the hi-fi systems came in so many different parts and were so awkward and cumbersome to put together. As one former hi-fi enthusiast says: 'I remember saving up to buy each little part. It took me about two years to collect all the different elements needed to connect it all together. Then I spent hours and hours trying to figure out where the wires went, as each part had its own components. When I finally finished it was a monstrosity in my living room that could never be moved no matter what.'

But Sugar came up with the perfect solution. He realized that many of the parts were unnecessary and only served to drive up costs. Furthermore, he knew that if he could get rid of these parts and make the hi-fi into an all-in-one system, then he could be onto a winner. So, in the late 1970s, the Amstrad Tower System was born.

It was a simple idea but ingenious at the same time. The Tower System comprised of a record player, cassette recorder/player and radio, all in one box. In true Amstrad signature style, the whole façade looked impressive and expensive. The whole system only needed one plug and it was ready to go. No longer did you need a Masters in engineering or copious amounts of time on your hands to get your hi-fi up and running. Now, anybody could own a hi-fi and tune into their favourite music within seconds.

KNOW YOUR MARKET

Back then, Sugar didn't use focus groups or formally carry out any real market research. He instinctively knew what his target consumer wanted because he was one of them. The early years he spent wheeling and dealing from the back of a van was experience that he couldn't have learned at university. During that time he was able to hone his sales patter, get to know the important retailers and study the products they were selling. It was these instincts that would make him a multi-millionaire.

However, he also knew how important it was not to rest on his laurels for any significant periods of time. His aim was for Amstrad to keep one step ahead of the market at all times. Indeed, when fashions changed or trends moved on, it was Amstrad that was first to the market with something new and innovative that would fly off the shelves. As there was very little bureaucracy and office politics in the early Amstrad days, decisions could be made instantly and production lines would start work immediately, sending products to retailers with breathtaking speed. No other competitor at the time was able to move with such speed and agility, and Amstrad reaped the benefits.

Sugar was able to produce a machine with an innovative design, take on the big boys in the technology industry and sell the computers all over the world.

But Sugar also knew when a product had had its day. There might be a radio that had done really well for a few months, selling in high volumes, but Sugar would sense a change in fashion, and simply take it off the market and produce something else in order to meet the next demand. As Gulu Lalvani, one of Sugar's first business role-models, said: 'Alan smelt, I mean smelt, that the market was on the point of going down. And his reaction was incredibly sharp.'

Sticking to this theory, by 1980, Amstrad was selling all manner of products: in-car entertainment systems, amplifiers, clock radios, Tower Systems and televisions. In a few short years, Amstrad had managed to come out of nowhere and take over the technology world, but Sugar was not content with his success and constantly sought out bigger and better things. When the computer industry caught his eye, he knew that he had found the challenge he had been looking for. With his finely tuned instincts, he knew that the market was ripe for a computer revolution and that he would be the one to lead it.

REVOLUTIONIZE YOUR WORLD

Before Amstrad, it was often the case that a home computer needed a separate cassette player and a television in order for it to work. Therefore, there was many an evening where family rows would ensue as to whether the evenings should be spent watching the television or playing the computer. It was usually the parents that wanted to tune into their television programmes, and the children who would want to use their computer, but usually the TV enthusiast would prevail. After a while, the rows would peter out and the computer would be shoved under the bed, never to be seen again.

Sugar had a solution to all of this. He understood that most people didn't want the hassle of putting together lots of cables and cassette decks, which they then had to connect to the TV in order for the computer to work. The Amstrad way was to make the experience much simpler, and so Sugar set about creating an all-in-one machine that could be used by anyone who had an interest in computing.

As usual, Sugar had thoroughly investigated the potential of an Amstrad computer and had ensured the product was viable. He bought various different types of machines made by competitors (on sale, of course) and took them apart to educate himself about the technology. He quickly realized that there was no big mystery to manufacturing computers and was inspired to produce a new, less complicated model, targeted for the mass market, at an afford-able price. By doing his homework, Sugar was able to produce a machine with an innovative design, take on the big boys in the technology industry and sell the computers all over the world. In doing so, he revolutionized the entire computer industry.

Because the new Amstrad CPC (Colour Personal Computer) was, again, an all-in-one piece, there was no danger of fighting between parents and their children. The children now had a sepa-rate machine of their own to play computer games, allowing their parents to watch television in peace. However, Sugar did not only target his new product at young people, but also designed the computer with adults in mind. With men in particular, he knew that size mattered, and built his computer to proportion, with the usual impressive, expensive-looking façade.

Once again, with his first computer model, Sugar had followed the Amstrad philosophy to the letter. He had innovated an existing product to appeal to his target market – the man on the street – stripped out all the unnecessary computer components, turned it into an all-in-one, simple-to-use device, given it a good polish, set it at an affordable price (thereby undercutting competitors) and sent it off to retailers to be sold to the awaiting public. However, later models were targeted at small businesses, or people that worked from home.

The genius of Amstrad's business model was that it catered for people who did not even know that they needed a product. For example, hi-fis were, traditionally, for the elite, as were the more highbrow, expensive computers. In his own words, he believes that he brought 'computing to the people who never even thought they would use a computer.'[3]

Indeed, many have observed that Sugar was a product of the Thatcher era. During the Thatcher years there was already a backlash against elitism, meritocracy and the Establishment. In many respects, Sugar was a model for the new prime minister: a working class lad that had left school at 16, and grafted to make his business a success.

Before Amstrad came along, the working classes had seldom given products like hi-fis and computers a second thought, as they were regarded as a luxury – expensive and unnecessary. However, Amstrad not only made it possible for the working classes to own these items, but also made 'luxury' more socially acceptable. Owning a computer or hi-fi was no longer frowned upon as a waste of good money, but soon became the norm, at first in the UK, and then all over the world.

Digital Retro author and technology writer Gordon Laing agrees that the Amstrad computer made technology more accessible and affordable for people: 'It represented fantastic value at a time when an IBM compatible or a Mac would cost a comparative fortune – that's why they were so popular with students and authors. I'm guessing it went the way of all non-IBM compatibles. The fact is proper PCs became affordable.'[4]

In short, Sugar had succeeded in democratizing these products across thousands of households and businesses.

ALWAYS LOOK FOR THE NEXT BIG THING

About three months after the launch of the first Amstrad computer, the Amstrad boss was becoming, characteristically, restless. He wanted to sink his teeth into a new project but was not sure where he could next turn his attention. Then it hit him.

It is believed that the typewriter has been around since the early 1800s. Widely used in offices worldwide, it was also bought for home use. The typewriter was a piece of history that nobody thought to tinker with – until Sugar came on the scene, of course. Word processors were in use around the UK but only the largest firms were able to afford them. So Sugar set himself yet another challenge: to produce a low-cost word processor for the masses.

Unsurprisingly, the reinvented typewriter (named the PCW) was a massive success, winning Sugar a huge amount of praise from the City and his peers. Stanley Kalms, then chairman of Dixons, said at the time: 'It was one of the great phenomenal take-offs in my experience ... Every secretary in every small company went to her boss and said: "I want one."' [5]

Sugar may have been blessed with an acute business instinct when it came to spotting the next big thing, but it was not instinct alone that ensured his products reached the market at the right place at the right time. Although he had graduated from his 'man-in-a-van' sales role, with honours, he never lost touch with what the consumer wanted. Before bringing any new product idea to fruition, he made sure he did his market research, studied consumer trends, and, more importantly, listened to what his customer wanted. His philosophy sounds simple – cater for the people who are buying your products – but it is amazing how many businesses today forget about their target audience and end up making products that fall flat in the marketplace.

Nowadays, the Amstrad ads are regarded as classics, and rightly so.

So although Sugar had designed his products with his consumers in mind, he also needed to advertise them effectively, in such a way that his consumers would also agree that Amstrad had indeed come up with 'the next big thing'. Although Sugar didn't fully believe in shelling out thousands of pounds on advertising, he did have a knack for creating ads that would capture the attention of his target market. The Amstrad style of advertising was honest, direct and straightforward; a sort of does-exactly-what-it-says-on-the-tin approach. They were cleverly constructed and used words that everybody could understand. Most advertising was done in-house with the boss, himself, having the final say.

The ad for the Amstrad PC 1512 was particularly clever and effective: 'How much computer can you buy for £450?' asks the headline. Then it shows images of other computers produced by major competitors such as Compaq, Olivetti and IBM, and shows how Amstrad's computer is better value all around. The ad concludes with a very neat message and a playful dig at his competitors: 'The Amstrad PC 1512. Compatible with you know who. Priced as only we know how.'

The ads for the PCW word processor were similarly creative. The image showed lots of beaten-up typewriters in a scrapyard, with the line: 'If you want to update your office, here's a tip.' The message could not have been clearer; it urged the customer to keep up with the times and get rid of their old, battered typewriters, and make way for the word processor – a machine that would revolutionize their working life.

These days, companies would spend huge amounts of money on advertising agencies just to produce ads as simple and as clever as these. The Amstrad ads are regarded as classics, and rightly so. Simple, effective and honest, they were able to draw in the customer time and time again.

Unlike many other competitors such as IBM and Apple, Sugar was not interested in building Amstrad as a brand. In fact, when Sugar was once asked if there was a Sugar brand, he famously retorted, 'Yes, Tate & Lyle.' With so many changing products and different markets, there was no point in pigeonholing the company into just one area. So Sugar focused on building awareness of Amstrad's products instead. However, whether he liked it or not, Amstrad had already become a brand. Indeed, the name itself is so catchy that it seems as if brand consultants were involved in creating it.

Sugar's talent for innovation and his ability to design a product had started to make huge waves in the marketplace. Indeed it was not surprising when, at the age of 37, he was awarded the prestigious Guardian Young Businessman of the Year, the first of many accolades. A revolution had begun.

START A REVOLUTION

With his uncanny instinct for spotting a market trend and keen eye for detail, Sugar managed to crash through class barriers with his low-cost, value for money products and no-nonsense advertising. Being innovative requires a creative mind but also an ability to take calculated risks. The 1980s were truly a golden era for Amstrad, which was fast becoming a force to be reckoned with.

- **Do your homework.** When it came to reinventing products, Sugar used all his resources to find out how that product was made and how he could do it better. This 'hands-on' approach was invaluable as it helped him to ascertain the features that would appeal to his target market.
- **Innovation is everything.** Innovation is key to the success of any business. Sugar saw that there was potential to innovate in the technological world and he grasped the opportunity with both hands.
- **Know your market.** Thanks to his days as a salesman, Sugar was able to get to grips with the demands of the man on the street and, later, the man in the office. He could also foretell when fashions and market trends were about to change, and be first with a product that would cater for these changes and meet market demand.
- **Revolutionize your world.** Sugar brought 'luxury' items such as computers, hi-fis and world processors to the masses. At the same time, he broke down social barriers and created the 'Amstrad effect', which rippled through much of society.

- **Always look for the next big thing.** Never one to rest on his laurels, Sugar has always turned his attention to what could be the next big thing. Through extensive research, listening to his customer and simple but effective advertising, Sugar's products always hit the right note.

3

KNOW YOUR CUSTOMER

'I struck my first business deals on the streets of Clapton as a 12-year-old boy by collecting lemonade bottles for the 1p deposits, and sitting on the main road asking for a penny for the guy.'[1]

– Alan Sugar

Alan Sugar has described himself as a salesman on many an occasion and he has the business success to prove it. However, a great salesman must be able to sell to anyone and relate to people from all walks of life – a talent displayed by Sugar from a very early age.

His love of the hard sell began when he was only a child, where he would sell bottles of homemade ginger beer to his thirsty schoolmates, his first real customers. In his teens he earned a few pence boiling beetroot for the local greengrocer, and helped out on a market stall, selling linens and fabrics. Even back then, he showed a great instinct for what people wanted and what they would buy. For example, he used to take black and white photos of families and sell them to the doting parents and grandparents for half a crown.

At school, his sales abilities caught the eye of his headmaster, who was both amused and surprised at the young Sugar's sales pitch in trying to persuade the headmaster to invest in a printing machine so the boy could start a school magazine. The headmaster was won over by the young boy's nerve and determination and, sure enough, the schoolboy got what he wanted – a pattern that would continue throughout his later career.

The young Sugar also took on a variety of Saturday jobs, one of which was selling shoes in a department store in Hackney. They were so impressed with his selling skills that they asked him to join them on a permanent basis. But the young entrepreneur had different ideas, and would soon apply his selling skills to bigger and better things.

Whether it was his schoolmates, managers of local small businesses or even authority figures like his headmaster, the young Sugar had the confidence and zeal to approach each and every one of them with his business propositions. His business pitches were delivered with both logic and passion, which both bemused and appealed to his listeners. With such honesty and sincerity, it is little wonder that the young Sugar managed to win over his audience time and time again.

READ YOUR CUSTOMER

So, how did he do it? How did the impoverished young lad from east London become such a huge success from his selling techniques? Selling is an art in itself; it is not as easy as it looks but getting the hang of it can make the difference between success and failure. To many of us, the art of selling is really intimidating, because we associate selling with bothering people. But it is important to remember that it is not just a product you are selling, but yourself. Sugar's gift for selling comes from experience and knowing not just what people want but about how people think and behave. He is a big fan of body language and his ability to read people is one of his greatest talents.

His love of the hard sell began when he was only a child.

Even at a young age, he had the uncanny ability to understand the psychology of the customer. One of his first partnerships as a teenager was with a television engineer called Malcolm Cross. They were in business for less than a year but during that time, they achieved quite a bit of success selling on reconditioned televisions to the public. Sugar came from a background where the television was still seen as a luxury, but the repaired models he sold were cheap and appealed to the working class, even if they did break down now and then. However, what was clever about the young Sugar's sales technique was how he positioned the product. He would just put one of the television sets out on display in his bedroom and tell the customer that it had been a gift to the Sugar family and they didn't want it anymore. That way, the customer would think there was only one available and would be more reluctant to walk away from the deal in case he missed out. Of course, unbeknown to the customer, there was a whole stack of patched-up tellies hidden from view, and the television that had been sold would be quickly replaced to sell to the next punter.

This is a technique that is used by retailers and businesses the world over, which are designed to appeal to our own sense of urgency. Shops regularly use a 'Closing Down Sale' to attract more consumers and get rid of stock. If the customer thinks they won't have another opportunity to buy the goods, they are more likely to spend money on the spot. Of course, more often than not, the shop really isn't going out of business and the whole thing is merely a marketing ploy to entice people into buying the stock.

One of the most valuable lessons that Sugar teaches in *The Apprentice* is to stay sharp and focused, and never let your mind wander from the bottom line.

Sugar seemed to understand from an extremely young age that customers needed to feel special, that the products are designed with them in mind, and want to feel that they are being given an exclusive deal.

However, no matter what technique Sugar used to make a sale, he always, *always* kept his eye on the bottom line – that all-important net profit figure that appears on an income statement after costs and expenses have been deducted from sales. That was his motivation – not to get too carried away by the sales he made because it was the profit that counted.

Thus, Sugar believes that profit margin is fundamental to business success: this is a message he constantly reiterates to the contestants in every series of *The Apprentice*. It sounds simple, but business is about making money. When people are caught up in a product, they tend to let emotions or their willingness to please others to get in the way, which leads them selling the product at a loss rather than a profit. One of the most valuable lessons that Sugar teaches in *The Apprentice* is to stay sharp and focused, and never let your mind wander from the bottom line.

TRUST YOUR INSTINCTS

Some people, Sugar included are just natural born salespeople. They can sell ice to Eskimos, sand to Arabs and pastries to the Danish. But the good news is that sales skills can be learned, lessons that Sugar teaches his apprentices during every series. Sugar is very upfront about his lack of academic skills and even admits to failing aptitude tests for jobs he applied for at IBM and ICL when he was 16 years old. Given that he would be directly competing with IBM only a decade later, perhaps failing that test was the best thing that ever happened to the young Alan Sugar. So a higher education helps, but it doesn't necessarily mean you will become a great salesman; selling is a skill like any other and requires time, commitment and more importantly practice in order to get just right.

Of course, some are better than others at selling. In Series 4 of *The Apprentice*, Michael 'Born to Sell' Sophocles raced after a reluctant bystander who had made the giant mistake of expressing a modicum of interest in leasing a Ferrari for a few hours. Not only had Sophocles misjudged his market by parking the car in an area not known for its stupendous wealth, but he proceeded to badger the poor customer until he physically had to run away from the over-eager salesman. The lesson here is to read the customer and know when to walk away. The majority of *Apprentice* viewers watching Sophocles in action would have known that the man was not in the least bit interested, and were most likely shouting at the television, telling Sophocles to leave the man alone!

There is a difference between determination and pushiness. A customer may buy a product just because they are intimidated into a purchase by the salesperson, but they will never return to the shop. The key is finding a balance between making the sale and not putting off the customer, which takes plenty of instinct and lots of determination.

Jenny Maguire from Series 4 infamously claimed to be 'the greatest saleswoman in Europe'. Consequently, she spent the entire time she was there trying to prove to Sugar, her fellow contestants and the viewing public that she was indeed as good as she said she was. Unfortunately, she didn't do enough to convince the boss, and she was fired in week 7.

One sales executive recalls, with some embarrassment, how she had also 'done a Maguire' and boasted to her boss that her sales instincts were so brilliant that she could sell anything to anyone, no matter what. When her boss took her up on the challenge, she found herself in a rather sticky situation:

> *'He told me to pretend I had to sell ice to Eskimos and gave ten minutes to plan my pitch. My boss then took on the*

role of the Eskimo and fired dozens of difficult questions at me. I was like a rabbit in the headlights and couldn't answer half of the questions. In hindsight, I realized that he was trying to gauge if there was any substance behind my bold statement, while also seeing how I would fare under pressure. Needless to say, I didn't do very well and was put firmly back in my box. But I definitely learned from the experience!'

GET YOUR HANDS DIRTY

Selling is all about getting stuck in and going that extra mile to close a deal. Sugar knows everything there is to know about getting his hands dirty. From selling beetroot to making ginger beer, the young Alan Sugar was not afraid of doing whatever was necessary to make his pocket money. When Sugar bought his first van, he would drive for hundreds of miles every day in order to sell electrical goods to eager retailers. This level of personal contact meant that Sugar was able to network with others in the field, gaining more knowledge about the retail world, the products they wanted and the ins and outs of how technology worked.

In *The Apprentice*, Sugar makes no pretence about the fact that he also likes his apprentices to get their hands dirty – literally.

When Sugar launched Global Audio, his first electronics shop, in north London with his partner Ashley Morris, he would frequently pop in, have a chat with the staff and start selling to customers. This wouldn't have been so unusual for a shop owner, but Sugar had agreed from the first instance that Global Audio would simply be a sideline for him – the ambitious entrepreneur was more or less happy to leave the day-to-day running of the shop to his partner and some extra staff. However, he couldn't resist dropping by on occasion and checking out his new venture. But he also had an ulterior motive: keeping his hand in allowed him to stay in touch with the people on the street – his target market, the real customer – making sure he was aware of market changes and shifting demands.

In *The Apprentice*, Sugar makes no pretence about the fact that he also likes his apprentices to get their hands dirty – literally. Over the last five series, the apprentices have been involved in tasks such as washing cars, doing laundry, selling flowers and fruit and veg, and generally liaising with the man on the street in order to get closer to the most important person in selling: the customer. From his vast experience, Sugar knows that the only way a product will meet the customer's needs is if the customer wants it in the first place. Therefore, by doing these tasks, the apprentices are learning a valuable lesson in business: to always stay in tune with their customer base. A retail salesperson agrees:

> 'The only way to keep in touch with your customer is by staying on the ground and really listening to what the customer wants. At our clothing store, we take feedback very seriously and always go that extra mile to satisfy our customer base. For example, if a customer asks whether we have a certain piece of clothing in a different colour or size, and we don't have it in stock, then we order it in for them. Furthermore, if the garment simply doesn't come in that particular colour or size, we actually put in a request to have it manufactured and delivered to the store specifically for that one customer. This strategy has allowed us to expand our retail outlets all over the world.'

GO ONE STEP FURTHER

Creativity and imagination can be powerful tools when it comes to making a sale, and Sugar picked up many tricks of the trade when he was in business. In the early 1970s, Amstrad had begun to manufacture parts for the audio industry and Sugar was looking for a retail outlet to help sell the products, with a particular interest in promoting Amstrad's new line of amplifiers.

In *The Amstrad Story*, David Thomas describes an instance which really illustrates the zeal and determination of the young Alan Sugar when it came to making a business deal with a much bigger player. Comet was *the* mega-electrical goods store at the time, and Sugar wanted their business. After weeks of persistence, Sugar managed to get an interview with Comet's marketing director, Gerry Mason. Mason agreed to do some business with Amstrad but wasn't in any way interested in selling the amplifiers in Comet's regional outlets. But the young entrepreneur was not satisfied with the deal, and haggled endlessly with Mason to at least put Amstrad's amplifiers onto Comet's mailing list. Mason agreed and, sure enough, the next time Comet published its listings, the Amstrad name was included.

But the determined youth wasn't finished yet. As soon as the Amstrad name appeared on the listings, he mobilized the troops and contacted family and friends from all over the country, asking them to each place an order for the amplifier. A week later, he got a call from Comet's head office, who were impressed with the immediate demand and requested that Amstrad send over more amplifiers. But Sugar was not celebrating just yet. Despite his big plans, Comet only wanted ten more – not even nearly enough to make an impact. In typical Sugar-style, he told head office what they could do with their ten amplifiers: 'Don't be so bloody stupid.

You're supposed to be Comet. I'm not selling you ten of anything. You've got to take at least 100 or it's ridiculous.'[2]

A short while later, the phone rang again. This time, Comet agreed to take 100 amplifiers off his hands. A few years later, reflecting on this event, Sugar said, 'We've never looked back. We've done mega-millions of pounds of business with them. But that's how it all started. That's how I broke into Comet. I conned them into it really.'

Sugar's early 'con' was a masterstroke that ended up forming a lucrative relationship with one of the UK's leading electrical retailers and earning him millions to boot. This was a real coup for the young entrepreneur and it really gave him the confidence to continue selling his products to other interested parties. Again, he had learned an important lesson: in selling, there is always that requirement to go one step further.

For many people, it would have been enough just to get a foot in the door with their target company, but Sugar went to the next level, enrolling his trusted contacts to place orders so he could prove to Comet that his products were popular with the public. Perhaps if he had waited and not enlisted the help of his family and friends, orders might have come in anyway and Comet would have realized that Amstrad was a force to be reckoned with. However, Sugar, then as now, was not known for his patience and wanted to drive the business forward with Comet. He succeeded tenfold, and never looked back.

PERSONALITY COUNTS

It sounds pretty simple but most people will buy from somebody that they actually like. An appealing personality and a fair degree of charm and sincerity can go a long way towards closing a deal.

Sugar may be tough but he also has a sense of humour and a refreshing honesty that appeals to his target market. Selling is about leaving your ego at the door and really listening to what the customer wants.

Sugar has always had a knack for building relationships and finding common ground with others.

Being as natural as possible, especially when delivering sales pitches, is a way of engaging the audience. Learning a sales patter word for word just comes across as unnatural, rehearsed and lacking in sincerity, and will not win over the target customer. The key to making a good pitch is to convey the information quickly and concisely. Customers can spot an insincere 'bluffer' from a mile away, so when selling, irrespective of what the product is, honesty and integrity are certainly the best way to get a sale.

Sugar has always had a knack for building relationships and finding common ground with others, which made it easier to make sales. Robert Hoban, Senior negotiator and salesman for a major country house auctioneers, agrees that the common ground approach is the most effective way to engage potential buyers:

> 'There are lots of important aspects to being not merely a salesman, but a good salesman. For me though, the most important of all is the ability to quickly and sensitively find common ground with the subject of your dealings. Ultimately, all sales transactions boil down to the human interaction between two people. In the case of selling property, in particular country houses, there are new encounters on a daily basis with potential purchasers, potential sellers, current clients, solicitors, bankers and numerous other members of the general public. They are all strangers with whom you have a short space of time

to get to know, find out what they are looking for and be in a position to provide it. You have to speedily succeed in making them feel at ease with you, feel comfortable sharing information with you, establish empathy and trust that you are on their side.'

Sugar's manner is as unscripted as it gets. He is a natural public speaker, who uses very few notes, and it is this talent as an orator that makes him very much in demand for public speaking engagements at universities, schools and businesses all over the country. Similarly, there are no scripts involved in *The Apprentice*; what you see is what you get, and that is enormously appealing for viewers and apprentices alike.

Sugar has more than 40 years of experience in the business world and in that time he has been able to identify his own strengths and weaknesses. This is the essence of a great salesman: someone who knows what they are good at but also works on the areas that need improvement. As the apprentices know only too well, acquiring much-needed sales experience is all about being taken out of your comfort zone. For example, you may be great at selling over the phone, but clam up during face-to-face selling; or you may be excellent at presenting and doing sales pitches in front of an audience, but totally clueless when it comes to actually closing a deal. Practice is the best way to achieve a top sales technique, something that is drummed into Sugar's apprentices week after week.

Ultimately, all sales transactions boil down to the human interaction between two people.

Ruth Badger ('The Badger' as she has been nicknamed by the media) from Series 2 of *The Apprentice* is probably the most skilled salesperson to feature so far in the programme. Pleasant but not pushy, seriously determined but respectful, and armed with a quirky sense of humour, she went on to close deal after deal after deal, particularly excelling in the car sales and flat-letting tasks. Her ability to win over her customer and close deals impressed Sugar so much that he put her through to the final. A worthy runner up in 2006, Ruth Badger is now one of the most successful apprentices in the series; she now runs her own consultancy business and even presents a television programme *Badger or Bust*, where she shares her expertise with struggling companies.

On the other side of the coin was Nargis Ara, who successfully demonstrated how not to make a sales pitch during her disastrous attempt at trying to sell cat calendars on behalf of Great Ormond Street Hospital to buyers at Virgin Megastore. Her selling technique won her no favours with her target customer and earned her a firing from Alan Sugar, who was shocked at the poor product and the way she had conducted herself during the task.

Knowing the product inside out and being able to describe it in plain language is the key to drawing in the customer. Many of us will have been frustrated by the lack of knowledge displayed by a salesperson that is supposed to know everything about a certain product but has no idea whatsoever. Our questions are greeted with a 'computer says no' type of response, and we most likely leave the store empty-handed and none the wiser about the product in which we were interested in the first place.

Doing your homework really counts, whether you are selling banking products, cars, flowers or fruit and veg – if you don't have the personality to talk freely and naturally about what you are selling, then you won't make the sale.

KNOW YOUR CUSTOMER

With his tough but honest approach, coupled with absolute determination and total self-belief, Sugar has proved himself to be the ultimate salesman. Before he even entered his teens, the young Alan Sugar demonstrated a unique talent for sales. Not only did he have a natural instinct for business, but he was able to read people, and ascertain exactly what they wanted. It was these qualities that helped Sugar become one of the country's most successful entrepreneurs.

- **Read your customer.** There is no point in trying to sell something to someone who does not want it in the first place. Learn body language and know when to go in for the kill, or when to walk away.
- **Trust your instincts.** Sugar prides himself on his finely tuned instincts and his ability to sniff out a deal at a moment's notice. Many successful businessmen rely on their instincts when making tough decisions. Instincts are a very important part of selling and they should not be ignored.
- **Get your hands dirty.** Selling is all about going that extra mile. Sugar got stuck in at every opportunity and his efforts and perseverance paid off. Never be afraid to go to the next level to close a deal.
- **Go one step further.** By the time he reached his twenties, the young Alan Sugar knew that he would always have to go to the next level if he wanted to achieve large-scale success. Never one for sitting around and waiting for things to happen, he made sure that he actively pursued every opportunity to the very end.

- **Personality counts.** Although he admits to being 'belligerent' at times, Sugar is all too aware that there is nothing more important in sales than having a good personality. Customers will only buy from someone that they can relate to and will not be impressed by pushiness, insincerity, dishonesty or aggression.

4

STAY TRUE TO YOUR VALUES

'I'm a great believer in solid foundations that will last – and that will serve your family, your community and, by implication, your country and future generations.'[1]

– Alan Sugar

Success in business is very much dependent on a core set of business values that transcends monetary terms. There is no such thing as overnight success; nor is there a magical formula to follow when setting up a new company. A successful firm cannot grow out of power, wealth and force of will alone. It is dependent on support from many avenues: its employees, suppliers, retailers, manufacturers and even the media. Reputation is absolutely key to a company's success, and the way to build that reputation is by creating an office culture that is founded on a solid base of business values.

When Sugar founded Amstrad, he strove to create a company culture that was based around strong business principles. Of course, these values were based on personal beliefs; for example, he believed in hard work, reliability, integrity, discipline, a real determination to succeed, and being ethical and truthful. If his employees did not conform to this model, then they didn't last very long. However, many Amstrad employees stayed with the company for more than 30 years, which showed that they were willing to follow Sugar's set of core business principles to the letter.

Alan Sugar has been criticized for being too old-fashioned in his outlook when dealing with his apprentices, but it is difficult to be too critical of someone that has built up a technology empire from scratch and made it into a phenomenal success story. If this is the sort of result that comes out of traditional business values, then perhaps more companies would do well to adopt Sugar's business model.

Business values go far beyond simple financial gain. They are fundamental to a company's reputation, and poor business values can make or break a fledgling operation. There are many definitions of what is meant by business values, but, generally, it means values that ensure the well-being of the firm in the long-term, taking into account customer value, employee value, supplier value and societal value. From a very young age, Sugar understood the importance of personal and business values in order to build a good reputation, and he applied them to Amstrad with resounding success.

Daniel Stane, founder and director of The Acumen Company (a specialist in improving organizational performance, engagement and values-based leadership behaviour) says:

> *'Sir Alan Sugar has built his credibility on walking his talk, and taking a firm stand on the issues and principles he believes in. In organizations, integrity is often about whether we are doing the "right" thing or not. But by whom? Often this just gets watered down into whether we are following the rule book, the company line or complying with policy. Famous for his ability to speak his mind, yet trusted by corporations, governments and broadcasters worldwide, Sir Alan's success reminds us of the need to listen to our own values, and courageously stand up for what we hold to be true. In our developmental work with corporate leaders, it is this congruence between beliefs and behaviours that shines out as a critical, winning trait in those role models we see consistently inspiring confidence, engagement and trust in their people.'*

MAKE GOOD ON PROMISES

Time and time again, Sugar has stressed the importance of following through on commitments. He does not make promises lightly, and always ensures that he keeps his word on every commitment he makes, a lesson he learned as a young boy. As a teenager striking out on his own, it was fundamental that the aspiring entrepreneur was able to win the trust of others in order to develop his own business model.

From a very young age, Sugar understood the importance of personal and business values in order to build a good reputation.

There is another anecdote from *The Amstrad Story*, which really shows how honesty, guts and determination can really pay off. When Sugar was still a teenager, he approached Ronnie Marks, the boss of Premier Radio, an audio shop on Tottenham Court Road. He went into the shop, told Marks that he had just set up on his own and needed some goods on credit to sell to other retailers. It was understandable that Marks was a little sceptical in allowing this determined youngster to go off with some of his stock. Of course, Sugar refused to take no for answer, and eventually a deal was worked out between Premier Radio and the young entrepreneur, albeit on very stringent terms.

Over the months, the teenager proved that he could be trusted by consistently abiding by the terms agreed with Marks. As Marks later said, 'He always, always honoured his obligations.' As he was so impressed with the young Sugar's integrity and reliability, Marks relaxed the terms of the agreement and began to entrust more responsibility to the young businessman. Sugar's reputation for honouring his obligations spread; soon, other established wholesalers began to make deals with the determined entrepreneur. Later on, the electrical giant Comet agreed to sell Amstrad products and was immediately impressed at how reliable Amstrad was for keeping to delivery dates. In a world where reliability wasn't exactly top of the list for lower-end suppliers, Sugar's philosophy for keeping to his promises came as a refreshing change.

This was an important early lesson for Sugar: to always make good on promises and honour obligations. It was these sorts of values that differentiated him from the other 'likely lads' who were in the same business at the time and were regarded as unreliable, untrustworthy and dishonest. Thus, as Sugar proved, it is never too early to start building up a good reputation. Even as a teenager, Sugar worked hard at getting his name out there as a man who could be relied on to do business with. The contacts he made with suppliers, wholesalers and retailers ended up being the very same people he dealt with on a daily basis during the Amstrad days. If he had upset any one of these contacts as a young-ster, they would most likely have never done business with him again further down the line.

As Sugar proved, it is never too early to start building up a good reputation.

People always remember those that make false promises or 'try to pull a fast one'. Sugar knew that reputation was everything when building up a business and he worked tirelessly to ensure that he never ever let anybody down. He also had the insight to realize that upsetting people would get him nowhere, and he was careful not to burn too many bridges.

Speaking in the mid-1980s, Lord Young, former Secretary of State for Trade and Industry, praised the young entrepreneur for his strength and determination: 'He's one of a new breed of British entrepreneurs. I would like to see people like that as role models for young people coming into the business. I want people to say, "Damn it, if he can do it, I can!"' [2]

BE GOOD TO YOUR STAFF

It's not money that makes a business successful but its employees – the people who come to work every day and strive to reach a common goal. Sugar may have been a tough boss, but he believed in entrusting responsibility to his staff, and rewarding them for hard work. He expected the staff to embody his own personal values of hard graft and integrity. Typically, Sugar was as uncompromising about his work ethic as he was about other matters, and it was not a subject that was up for discussion; if an employee found it difficult to adhere to the boss's principles, it wouldn't be long before he was looking for another job.

Sugar may have been a tough boss, but he believed in entrusting responsibility to his staff, and rewarding them for hard work.

Being responsible for thousands of staff and a hugely successful business empire requires courage and sheer guts, especially when it comes to making tough decisions. When the livelihoods of the staff are on the line, it is crucial to choose the right path. From the outside, Amstrad gained a reputation for being one of the toughest companies to work for, headed up by the most intimidating boss. Indeed, Sugar once joked that his staff were lucky if he threw them a sandwich for lunch.

The Amstrad head office was a no-frills affair, an ugly building that wasn't much better inside. City businessmen were surprised at the level of austerity at the Amstrad offices, which were in stark contrast to the plush surroundings of their top financial firms. However, Sugar wasn't interested in window dressing and had neither the time nor the patience to decorate or choose sculptures to display in the lobby – his main focus was on his work and how his staff performed. Unusually for that era, Sugar sat at a desk among his staff. He didn't feel any need for a fancy office, preferring to be on the ground, calling the shots and directing his team.

Undoubtedly, Sugar had high demands on his staff and many were terrified of his straight-talking, pull-no-punches attitude. However, a large number of his employees stayed at Amstrad for decades, and still speak highly of him today.

So the boss was not into giving anyone a free ride but once they earned their stripes, they were accepted into the culture and were always treated fairly. Sugar made sure that his staff were rewarded for their work by giving them share options, which meant that they felt like they were a real part of the success of Amstrad. As he would do many years later in his speeches to young people, he also inspired his employees to do better, to continue to reach their goals and to take pleasure in success. He really made them feel that they were a part of something big, not just a corporate cog in the wheel. It was this managerial approach that ensured loyalty from his staff, and their willingness to stay at Amstrad for years and years reflects their fondness and respect for their gruff boss.

GIVE SOMETHING BACK

Unlike other celebrities and top businessmen, Sugar has been very quiet about his charity work. When Amstrad began to take off, Sugar was very keen to give something back and to help others in difficult situations as much as he could. A key element of his core set of business values was the duty he had towards society.

Running a large company is not purely dependent on the responsibility you have for your staff or your clients, there is also a duty to society. Alan Sugar embraced his societal values as a young businessman and has always been keen to give something back to the community.

He has long been a patron of the Hackney Empire theatre, where he has donated huge sums of money in order to restore it to its former splendour. Of course, Hackney is where Sugar was born and where he grew up – the place where he made his first marks on the business world – so the Hackney Empire was one building he could not let fall into disrepair. However, Sugar has not just limited his generosity to his local community: through his own charitable company The Alan Sugar Foundation, which he set up in 1986, he has also been a generous benefactor of Great Ormond Street children's hospital and Jewish Care. The charity has donated millions of pounds to charitable concerns, including an old people's home and a high school, and has raised almost £200,000 for the Muscular Dystrophy Group.

In 1993, he was one of the founders of the government-run Excalibur Scholarship Scheme, which involved raising money to help finance graduates from the old Eastern Bloc to study in Europe. In 1997 Sugar was asked by Gordon Brown, then chancellor of the Exchequer, to join the 'You can do it too' scheme to promote the values of enterprise amongst young people. This led to Sugar touring the country, talking to young people and inspiring them to start up their own businesses. It was his gift for public speaking and his ability to get through to young people that attracted wide audiences to his speeches. Eventually, TV executives also spotted his gift as an orator and believed he was a natural choice for the UK version of *The Apprentice*.

In recognition for his charitable work, Sugar received the title of honorary doctor of science from City University Business School and was awarded the same title from Brunel University. The man that left school at 16 now has two degrees from prestigious universities. He is also chairman of the governors at King Solomon High School and honorary chairman of Bristol University Enterprise Centre.

> **'You go into the Alan Sugar school of management and you get the fat worked off you.'**

However, it was in 2000 that he received the highest accolade of his career. Alan Sugar from Hackney, east London, became the rather grand-sounding Sir Alan Sugar. Finally, he had been officially recognized by the country he loved: not just for being one of the UK's most successful entrepreneurs, but also for the time and money he had invested in his charity work.

However, Sugar's run of recognition didn't just end there. In 2009 he was offered the role of 'enterprise czar' in the House of Lords, and became Lord Sugar; and is now named as Baron Sugar of Clapton in the London Borough of Hackney. In his new role, he acts as an official adviser to the Prime Minister on how to help support struggling small businesses especially during the economic downturn. Like many of his roles outside the business world, Sugar gives his time for free. Indeed, the fee he earns for his appearance on *The Apprentice* goes straight to charity.

Sugar's commitment to giving something back to the community does not just involve financial contribution, but also an investment of his own time. Rather than just throwing money at a cause and walking away, in typical Sugar-style, he is happy to get stuck in and get his hands dirty, and really strives to achieve real results. It is clear that Alan Sugar is as driven when it comes to charity work as he is in business, a quality that is quite rare among wealthy celebrities.

CHOOSE FAMILY OVER PROFIT

These days, it is not unusual to work long hours; many employees end up eating dinner at their desks. Indeed, Microsoft employees regularly burn the midnight oil, ordering pizzas to the office to stave off hunger. Alan Sugar has always been a family man. He met his wife, Ann, when he was 17 and she was 16, and they married a few years later. Although he was a man that was, undeniably, addicted to building up his empire, he always made sure that he didn't let business get in the way of his family life.

Indeed, from a very young age, Sugar was always a great believer in a work-life balance. A firm advocate of both working and playing hard, as soon as the office doors closed, he would try not to bring his work home with him, but spend the rest of the evening with his family instead. Often when he is asked the secret of his success, he credits his family for his achievements, advising other aspiring entrepreneurs, 'Put your loved ones, not your profit margin, centre stage.'[3] The Amstrad office was firmly shut at 5.00 p.m. (which is pretty early by today's standards) and employees were informed to either leave the building or risk getting locked in.

Later on, when he started making his real fortune, he was determined not to let his new-found wealth go to his head or have an adverse effect on his children. He made sure that they learned the value of money and encouraged them to get part-time jobs, to earn a crust for themselves. One of his sons, Simon, worked at McDonalds for a few months, and his other son Daniel also had a number of jobs. When they were old enough, both sons joined Amstrad in different roles, but were given no special favours by the boss. Again, both sons needed to embrace their father's business ethos in order to make their mark in their respective roles. However, Sugar is no stranger to the politics involved when hiring family members. He even employed his own father when his business started to take off.

It is clear that Alan Sugar is as driven when it comes to charity work as he is in business.

Again, the message is very clear: whether employing family or the man off the street, the most important thing is that everybody works hard towards achieving success for the company; after all, if the company takes off, then everybody benefits.

Sugar was adamant that his children would not be spoiled by his wealth. Many children from wealthy backgrounds tend to grow up in a 'trust fund' environment, in which they feel they can have anything they want without having to work for it. These children eventually grow up spoilt and lazy, with little purpose in life and are the more miserable for it. Sugar has never forgotten his roots and, although his children never had to graft the way he did, he certainly feels a moral commitment towards teaching them the value of money. Indeed, his daughter Louise remembers how she would have to go to both her parents as a child and explain the reasons why she deserved her pocket money that week – which was probably one of her first business pitches! Either way, whether it was an employee or a toddler, Sugar wasn't about to give away money to those that didn't deserve it.

Sugar is also a strong believer in keeping his business and personal life separate. There were only two occasions in his career that led to a mingling of the two. The first was very much unwanted. It was not by choice that Sugar's involvement with Tottenham Hotspur led to a persecution of his family. His unpopularity with the Spurs fans resulted in protesters picketing outside his house, and making death threats to himself and his family. It was the impact on his family that encouraged Sugar to step down as chairman of the football club, after ten years of service. It is not a time that he looks back on fondly.

As much as Sugar cultivates his business ethos at work, he rates family values as the main reason for his success.

When Sugar mixed business with pleasure a second time, it was a far happier occasion. In May 2009, Sugar and his wife celebrated their fortieth wedding anniversary. Held in a marquee in the back garden of his lavish mansion in Chigwell, Essex, the party was attended by famous faces such as Bruce Forsyth, Jackie Mason and a whole host of other celebrities, coupled with a surprise performance from Elton John. For a man who has a reputation for being scary and aggressive, he is certainly very popular!

During the party, Sugar made a very humorous speech, cracking jokes and generally bringing the house down. He also spoke about that rather unfortunate, yet amusing, incident where he had absent-mindedly signed a birthday card to his wife, 'Best wishes, Sir Alan Sugar', which served as a reminder that he had become a little too caught up in his work that day. Then he moved on to a more serious note, and revealed the real secret of his success over the years:

> *'A real successful man puts the love of his wife and children first, a real successful man's greatest position in life is to have a great family … everything I have today is because of the love of that lady and the respect my three children have for the both of us.'*[4]

As much as Sugar cultivates his business ethos at work, he rates family values as the main reason for his success. For Sugar, the love and support and respect he received from his family helped to make him into the role model he is today. Although some may view his emphasis on the family as central to business success as a little old-fashioned, there is no denying that these traditional values have given him the strength and confidence to battle through the bad times, and turn failure into achievement.

STAY TRUE TO YOURSELF

Throughout his whole career, Sugar has always followed his own personal beliefs and values. He has never wavered from his responsibilities and had always attempted to do the right thing. Consistency of character is key when running a large organization. It is what makes others trust you and helps to build up relationships and loyalty.

As a youngster, Sugar already showed signs of his strength of character, his eagerness to work hard, and his distaste for letting others down. As he began to emerge as one of the UK's most promising entrepreneurs, heads started to turn in his direction. City businessmen arrived at Amstrad to make deals with this tough-talking young man, which captured the attention of the media, who in turn put him firmly under the spotlight. However, Sugar was never intimidated by this sudden attention and certainly never felt the need to adapt his behaviour or the way he carried out business. His personal values had been instilled in him from such a young age that he would have them for life.

Staying true to himself allowed him to remain confident in his own abilities and have the personal self-belief to make tough decisions. It is this unwavering strength of character, these strong business and personal values, and a strict work ethic that has made him into the success he is today.

STAY TRUE TO YOUR VALUES

From a young age, Sugar understood the importance of applying a core set of business values that he based on his own personal beliefs. Setting business principles is not just a corporate strategy, but involves an emotional as well as a practical investment. The success of a company very much depends on its leader and the example they set to their employees and others that they come into contact with. Through the support of his family, Sugar was able to build up a good company culture with an excellent reputation and develop an enterprise that was known for its integrity and reliability.

- **Make good on promises.** One of Sugar's chief business values was to always follow through on commitments and to never backtrack on a deal. He was careful not to make enemies, knowing that people have long memories and tend to hold grudges. He valued the business relationships he made and always made sure he kept his word on every promise he made.

- **Be good to your staff.** From the very beginning of his fledgling company, Sugar made sure his staff benefited from the company's success. He hired like-minded people who were grafters and had the determination to succeed. As the boss, he made them feel part of the success and thus secured their loyalty and commitment for many years.

- **Give something back.** Societal values are very important to Sugar. He is always keen to give something back to the community, and to the country that allowed him to build up a business from nothing. He gives generously to charity and is actively involved in a number of activities where he invests a great deal of his own time to help others, without demanding any payment, because he firmly believes it is the right thing to do.

- **Choose family over profit.** Married at a young age, Sugar has always been a family man and certainly prioritizes his wife and children over his work. He credits his family for making him the success he is today and has always striven to keep his personal and business lives separate.

- **Stay true to yourself.** Sugar has been in business for more than 40 years but despite his success and wealth, he never strayed from his own personal beliefs and values. He may have been criticized for being 'old-fashioned' and 'traditional', but these values allow him to be the role model he is today.

5

LEARN FROM YOUR MISTAKES

'All men make mistakes, but only wise men learn from their mistakes.'

– **Winston Churchill**

Like many successful entrepreneurs, Sugar has made his fair share of mistakes that have damaged both his wallet and reputation. Today, Sugar is a household name, extremely popular with both young and old, and riding high in public opinion. In fact, in a survey by Ipsos MORI carried out on behalf of Christian Aid, the British public voted Alan Sugar as their most preferred celebrity to take part in their quiz team, pipping housewife's favourite Terry Wogan to the post. However, the British public were not always so supportive of Sugar, and there was a time when he was one of the UK's most hated figures in the public eye.

DON'T FALL AT THE FIRST HURDLE

When Sugar first entered the business world at the tender age of 16, he understandably made his fair share of mistakes. Just after he had started out on his own, his entire stock was stolen from his family home, where he had been storing it. With no insurance and no way of getting the stock back, it was a bit of a setback for the young entrepreneur. However, he may have been down but he certainly wasn't out. Indeed, this incident merely served to provide him with an incentive to look for bigger and better premises to store his stock, and to take out the necessary insurance to protect his assets.

This was a valuable lesson for the aspiring entrepreneur, and shows how determined the young Alan Sugar was to make a success of his fledgling business. Many teenagers of that age would have thrown in the towel at this stage, and would not have been able to cope with such a devastating blow to their business. Similarly, others might blame the thieves for the collapse of the business and either seek retribution, or use the theft as an excuse for the failure of the company. However, Sugar's actions at this time are a testament to his determination and strength of character, qualities that would see him through some very tough times in the future.

KEEP YOUR EYE ON THE BALL

In 1991, Sugar and former football player and manager Terry Venables joined forces to rescue Tottenham Hotspur from the verge of bankruptcy. Again, Sugar had taken on the big boys to secure his prize, this time in the form of newspaper mogul Robert Maxwell, who was also keen to get involved in the club. As soon as the takeover battle was won and the deal was closed, Sugar rolled up his sleeves and got stuck in.

From the very beginning Sugar made it very clear that he viewed Spurs as a business venture only, and that his main focus was saving the club from sinking into debt. Indeed, one of the first moves undertaken by Sugar and his new partner Venables was to pay off the club's £20 million debt.

In 1993, Sugar was forced to make one of the toughest decisions in his career and it was Terry Venables that came into the firing line. But he could not have anticipated the backlash. Never one for caring about his popularity when it comes to business, even Sugar was shocked by the sheer vitriol displayed by the football fans. When he sacked Venables, all hell broke loose. Venables was a hugely popular figure and idolized by sports fans all over the country. As Sugar put it, 'I felt as though I'd killed Bambi'.

An ugly court case ensued with Sugar emerging the winner, but there were no victory celebrations. Instead, Sugar turned his attention back to the club and worked hard to

'I felt as though I'd killed Bambi'.

turn it back into the financially stable club it had once been. But the Spurs fans weren't going to forgive him so easily for getting rid of their idol and proceeded to harass Sugar and his family at every turn. Author and investigative journalist Graham Johnson remembers:

> 'Alan Sugar was hated when he was at Spurs. He treated it as a normal business, but the difference with football is that the consumers have a fanatical loyalty to the brand unlike any other business. They took his decisions personally and started protesting outside his house and making death threats, which came as a shock to him and his family. In addition, at the time, the culture of football was very aggressive. It was around the time when hooliganism was at its height. So it seemed natural to many supporters to react that way. But probably one of the most shocking things he discovered was that football isn't really a business. There's lots of debt. Many clubs don't really make a profit and there's little in the way of strategy. Management hierarchy is not a big deal. The players on the pitch and other club officials can often have more impact in the media and in the club than the chairman.'

In 2001, Sugar took stock of his ten years as chairman at Spurs, the strain it had put on himself and his family, considered the hundreds of death threats he received every day from Spurs fans – and walked away. He sold his majority stake in Spurs for £22 million, before selling the rest of his shares for £25 million in 2007.

Commenting on Sugar's time at Spurs, Bernie Kingsley of the Tottenham Supporters Trust said that he had mixed feelings about Sugar's departure: 'I'm not a rabid anti-Sugar man, but it's hard to deny that things haven't gone how they should since he's been in charge.'[1] But he also commented that Sugar had made a big difference when it came to sorting out the financial tangle at the club and remarked: 'I think the fans respect rather than like Sugar for that.' This is the essence of Alan Sugar: you don't have to like him but you can't help but respect him for what he has achieved.

You don't have to like him but you can't help but respect him for what he has achieved.

Oddly enough, the once-scorned Venables also has praise for the tough businessman: 'I don't know what would have happened to the club without him. He was the only one prepared to go through with it.'[2]

Although Sugar turned the financial future of the club around and made a huge impact on Spurs' standing in the world of sport, the constant harassment, pressure and legal battles eventually wore him down. He views his ten-year period as chairman as one of the darkest times in his career and, looking back, says that his decision to get involved in Spurs was 'a very bad move', a 'thankless, hopeless task', and that he 'wasted ten years of my life on that nonsense'.

However, perhaps he was being too hard on himself. Despite endless criticism and zero support from inside the club and out, for ten long years Sugar defiantly battled against the rising tide of negative public opinion to do what he had signed up for: to save the club from financial disaster. In typical Sugar-style, he had made a commitment and was damn sure going to see it through until the bitter end. A lesser man would have walked away a lot sooner than that. With characteristic grit and determination, Sugar trod a very rocky road and did what

Sugar trod a very rocky road and did what he had to do, but he also had the instinct to know when his time was up.

he had to do, but he also had the instinct to know when his time was up. Sugar can be assured of his achievements at Spurs and fully credited for saving a treasured British institution from disaster. Over the years, Sugar has since won the respect of his former adversaries who have acknowledged his role in saving Spurs. And thanks to his relatively recent foray into the media world, public opinion of Sugar has never been higher, making him one of the best-loved figures in the UK.

SADDLE UP AND RIDE OUT THE STORM

During the 1990s Sugar was heavily involved in Spurs, which distracted him from Amstrad. Looking back at this difficult period at Amstrad, Sugar admits that he had taken his eye off the ball with regards to the business world and hadn't paid enough attention to what was going on at the company he had founded. He admits that he is 'a one-trick pony'[3], meaning he can only focus on one business at a time, and his gruelling role as Spurs chairman had diverted his attention from the inner machinations of his own company.

However, things had started to go downhill at Amstrad a couple of years before Sugar joined Spurs. Suddenly, 'the Amstrad effect' had started to wear off. The late 1980s proved to be a challenging time for Amstrad. The stock market crash of 1987 heavily impacted the value of Amstrad, and it took a few years for the company to recover. In 1988 – or 'the year of disaster', as Sugar refers to it – the company made a £114 million loss in sales because it had failed to manufacture enough products to meet growing demand. Rather than surrendering to this seemingly insurmountable obstacle, Sugar took the opportunity to put aside his ego and took a step back to figure out what had happened and how it could be put right again.

Indeed, the massive financial loss was also down to circumstances outside the company's control. Memory chips, a vital component in manufacturing computers, were rising in price and in short supply, making it almost impossible to produce the machines. But Amstrad was not alone. The mighty Apple Computer organization also experienced a significant loss in profits as a result in the massive escalation in price for the chips. Sugar knew better than to sit around licking his wounds and hoping everything would work out for the best. So, he took decisive action to salvage what he could from the seemingly disastrous situation.

Sugar has, typically, been completely upfront about what happened and takes total responsibility for the mistakes made.

Amstrad bought a stake in Micron Technology, a provider of memory chips, and did a deal with Samsung to ensure a further supply of the crucial components. Although the deal with Micron turned out to be a costly risk in the end, it provided a solution to the memory chip debacle.

Labour shortages in Taiwan and production delays in Japan also heavily contributed to Amstrad's woes. The launch date of the two most expensive computers in the range was delayed by a lengthy seven months. However, when some of the newer models were about to be launched, it transpired that the machines were faulty – leading to a recall of 7000 of the models.

There was also trouble in subsidiaries in Spain and West Germany, where management bungled marketing pitches and mishandled inventory. Both mistakes had a massive impact on sales. Sugar took quick decisive action and swiftly discharged the heads of the operations in both countries – tough but necessary measures, typical of Sugar's management style.

However, things went from bad to worse and the City executives were beginning to doubt Sugar's ability to take control at the helm, their anxiety reflected in the plummeting share prices. But Sugar was determined to turn the situation around, rebuild Amstrad's image and restore investors' faith in the company and himself as a top-class entrepreneur.

Many top businessmen would blame extenuating circumstances for the weaknesses in their company, but Sugar has, typically, been completely upfront about what happened and takes total responsibility for the mistakes made: 'We expanded too quickly, and we screwed up. We didn't have enough understanding of the technology as it got more complex, and I take total responsibility for that.'[4]

In 2005, looking back on that troubled time at Amstrad, Sugar said, 'I blame myself for not having a wider vision, a longer-term view. I'm more of a short-term trader, I want to have it now, that kind of thing.'[5]

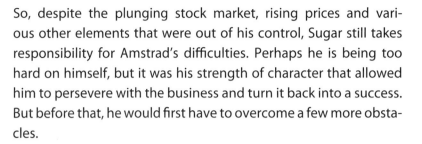

So, despite the plunging stock market, rising prices and various other elements that were out of his control, Sugar still takes responsibility for Amstrad's difficulties. Perhaps he is being too hard on himself, but it was his strength of character that allowed him to persevere with the business and turn it back into a success. But before that, he would first have to overcome a few more obstacles.

BACKING THE WRONG HORSE

The Amstrad team was overwhelmed by the fast expansion of the company and had started to make mistakes. New products were entering the market but were being slammed for poor quality and design. In September 1988, a new venture into the business market with the Sinclair-branded PC200 computer was heralded as 'Sugar's Christmas Turkey' in *PC Dealer* magazine. Two years later, the GX4000 games console was launched, but poor availability of software and competition from the impressive Sega Mega Drive was too fierce, and the GX4000 flopped as a result.

In 1993 Amstrad introduced the PenPad or PDA600, in an attempt to break into the handheld device market in the UK and Europe. It was, essentially, an electronic personal organizer that included functions such as calendar, address book, calculator, etc. Like many producers of pen computing products, including Apple, the Pen-Pad struggled to make a dent in the market and slowly faded into obscurity. It was not until 1996 when the PalmPilot was launched that pen computing would achieve phenomenal success. A later videophone that incorporated email as well as the phone also met with a similar fate.

However, although certain Amstrad products failed to achieve mass popularity, some of the reasons why they weren't selling as well as they should were genuinely out of Sugar's hands. In the late 1980s, there were very high expectations for the PC2386 and PC2286, Amstrad's new computer models that were to be targeted at small businesses as well as for home use. But the computers had to be recalled because of faulty hard disk drives. The cost of recalling and replacing the disks was high, but didn't compare to the damage done to Amstrad's reputation. Amstrad sued Seagate Technology, the company that was responsible for supplying the disks, and won, but by then it was too late.

Amstrad suffered a blow to its reputation but, ever the resolute businessman, Sugar picked himself up and dusted himself off, determined to introduce a new product that would capture the imagination of the public once more.

In later years, despite its frequent appearances on *The Apprentice*, Amstrad's e-m@iler failed to completely win over the public, who disliked being charged for checking email and for sending SMS messages.

The aim of the e-m@iler was to allow people to send email, text messages and carry out a whole host of other functions, without the need for a PC. Again, Sugar was catering for the mass market; those who wanted the basic facilities of a PC at a price they could afford. However, although the new all-in-one gadget received dubious customer reviews and scepticism from the press, the e-m@iler actually sold far more than the media let on – almost 298,000 units over four years, which is a pretty impressive result for a product that was, and still is, judged so harshly. However, with Sugar's usual instinct of knowing when to walk away, he finally pulled the plug on the e-m@iler in 2006. It had not been the glorious success that he had expected, but he would soon move on to bigger and better things.

SHUN SUGAR-COATING

Owning up to mistakes is one of the best ways to secure the respect of peers. Both the City financiers and the press were impressed by Sugar's honesty about the difficulties Amstrad had faced from 1988 to 1989. Roger Crowe, a reporter for *The Guardian*, wrote an article praising Sugar for accepting responsibility for Amstrad's drop in profits, and welcomed the business mogul's frank and honest approach.

The press were used to the head honchos of failing companies trying to cover up their mistakes or using confusing and ambiguous language to sugar-coat the reality. Sugar's upfront admission about what had triggered Amstrad's poor performance won him the respect of his former adversaries: the press and the City.

Sugar also learned a valuable lesson from the time he spent at Tottenham Hotspur. He realized that he had made a mistake in entering a business that he knew absolutely nothing about. Conversely, when building up Amstrad, Sugar had earned his stripes on the streets of east London, picking up the tricks of the trade and applying them to his own business. It was this sort of experience that allowed him to make the impressive transition from a man selling out of the back of a van to a hugely successful entrepreneur.

When addressing more than 300 people at the University of Oxford, Sugar told his captive audience to 'stick to what you know' in relation to his ten-year foray into football politics. It was a valuable lesson for the seemingly invincible businessman to learn: do your research before you jump in with both feet. Indeed, in 2005, he told *The Independent's* Sholto Byrnes that he would have 'done better going down to Hackney Community Centre talking to young kids every Saturday for ten years'. Clearly, Sugar felt his time at the football club would have been better spent mentoring young people rather than battling the bureaucracy of the sports world.

Both the City financiers and the press were impressed by Sugar's honesty about the difficulties Amstrad had faced from 1988 to 1989.

He has also learned to deal with the ups and downs of public opinion. There is no question that during the Tottenham Hotspur days Sugar went from being hailed as 'the man of the people' to 'the man most hated by a large proportion of the people'. But it wasn't just his activities as football club chairman that brought his popularity into question. Faulty Amstrad products and falling share prices attracted unwanted attention from the media who slated the entrepreneur on a regular basis, which caused a divide between Sugar and the press that remains today. Indeed, Sugar is well known for his (perhaps justified) mistrust of journalists and remains reluctant to talk to the papers or give interviews.

However, despite the bad times, Sugar weathered each storm with grace and dignity, together with a heavy measure of honesty and forthrightness. In an otherwise cut-throat business world, his ability to admit to his mistakes and accept responsibility certainly comes as a refreshing change.

LEARN FROM YOUR MISTAKES

Throughout his extensive career, Alan Sugar has made some good and not-so-good decisions. However, his total belief in learning from his mistakes has allowed him to recover from his various falls from grace, earning the respect from both his peers and the public. Today, Sugar's star is on the rise and his popularity, which transcends generations, knows no bounds.

- **Don't fall at the first hurdle.** Sugar's biggest mistake as a teenager starting out in business was to put all his eggs in one basket and store his entire stock at his own home, without any insurance. However, he learned a valuable lesson that led to him investing in new premises and seeking out advice as to how he could protect his assets. These are valuable lessons for any entrepreneur who is trying to build up his business.
- **Keep your eye on the ball.** Moving into an entirely new industry can be distracting, as Sugar discovered to his detriment. He admitted to taking his eye off the ball at Amstrad, during his years at Tottenham Hotspur, but it was time that wasn't wasted; he saved the club from financial ruin and walked away with his head held high.
- **Saddle up and ride out the storm.** Every business goes through its ups and downs, but the most important thing is to keep fighting and get back on top again. In the late 1980s, Sugar faced a whole range of issues at Amstrad from faulty products to false rumours, but he rode out the storm, emerging stronger than ever.

- **Backing the wrong horse.** Amstrad had a reputation for building innovative and value-for-money products that appealed to the mass market, and many were phenomenally successful. However, there was a period where Amstrad's products didn't sell as well as they should. Sugar did not see this as a sign to throw in the towel, but analyzed why the products had not taken off and put even more effort into further projects to ensure the same problems didn't occur again.
- **Shun sugar-coating.** Sugar's honesty and willingness to accept responsibility for mistakes has won the respect and admiration from his peers and the public. He refuses to sugar-coat his mistakes and prefers to be upfront about the problems he has experienced.

6

DRIVE A HARD BARGAIN

'He's very entrepreneurial, a tremendous worker. In negotiations, he's a master of detail.'[1]

– Rupert Murdoch

Like sales, negotiation is a skill that requires plenty of practice. It takes lots of confidence and an ability to stay calm, even in the most nerve-wracking situations. Many of us are afraid to negotiate for fear that we will fail, or even offend the other person. We may not realize it but negotiation is a part of everyday life, whether we are trying to get a pay rise or organizing a team to work on a project. Negotiation is about reaching an agreement with others (who may have different ideas and viewpoints) by seeking common ground through a give-and-take process. Typically, a good negotiator has excellent people skills, integrity, an open mind, preparation and planning skills, charisma, patience, good communication skills, and clear judgement.

Alan Sugar is as competitive as it gets and is famous for his tough negotiating skills. But rather than being feared for his negotiation style, he is actually admired. Indeed, many of his former business associates actually said that they found the Amstrad boss easy to deal with. 'Easy' isn't a word that some of us would normally attribute to someone like Alan Sugar, but when it comes to negotiation, he is straightforward, honest and always lets everybody know where they stand. Never afraid to cut through the jargon to get to the heart of a business deal, he makes sure that every meeting ends in a positive result for both parties. He may be a tough negotiator, but he is always fair, and never, ever reneges on his promises.

The media mogul Rupert Murdoch was particularly impressed with Sugar when he made a deal with him to manufacture a million satellite dishes in one year in preparation for the launch of Sky Television. This was one of Sugar's most successful deals and really proved what an excellent businessman he is. Amstrad and Sky enjoyed such a long, mutually beneficial relationship that in 2007, Sugar sold Amstrad to Sky for £125 million.

REACH FOR THE STARS

Fear of failure is one of the main reasons why people shy away from negotiating. However, it is vital to aim high and have a goal in mind before the negotiation process even begins. Like all entrepreneurs, Sugar has exceptionally high expectations and knows exactly how to get what he wants. Even as a young businessman, he would always aspire to get more out of every deal than what was on offer.

Aspiring to a seemingly impossible goal is one of the best qualities of a top entrepreneur. Without goals, there can be no successful end result; without a clear vision, there is a strong possibility that the deal will fall flat. So before the negotiation process begins, it is important to set your goals, have a vision and be completely clear about your objectives. If you don't have enough confidence in yourself or the product, others will pick up on it and use it to their advantage. Self-belief and confidence are absolutely key when trying to make a successful deal.

But there is no use having a vision or goals if they are not backed up by hard facts. Being prepared before going into a negotiation is the most important part of the process. The Pareto Principle states that if 20% of our time is spent on the issues that really matter, then it will achieve an 80% result. Thus, focusing on the planning process will reap long-lasting rewards.

Sugar always made sure he knew his facts and figures inside out, not just about his own business and products, but about the other party as well. This knowledge helped him to logically answer every single question that was thrown at him. The other party would eventually realize that this man with all the answers was worth doing business with!

Similarly, anybody on the cusp of entering negotiations with Sugar would be wise to do their research too, and even prepare a script or at least rehearse what they are about to say. Research would show them that Sugar doesn't suffer fools, despises insincerity or manipulative behaviour, and can't stand people that pretend to know more than they actually do. As we have seen in *The Apprentice*, Sugar can see straight through that sort of behaviour in the boardroom, and has no tolerance for it. He is an assertive negotiator (which some people confuse with aggression) and trying to imitate him by responding in an antagonistic manner wins no favours whatsoever.

Alan Sugar is as competitive as it gets and is famous for his tough negotiating skills.

Although Sugar has achieved so much in a head-spinning short period of time, he never let his ego get in the way or saw himself as the all-powerful one, or as the big boss calling the shots. He also knows the value of behaviour during the negotiation process and is aware that if others perceive him to be argumentative, aggressive and non-committal, no matter who he is, they will not enjoy doing business with him. Sugar embodies different types of power:

- Interpersonal power, which means he has a talent for communicating with people from all walks of life.

- Referent power, i.e. he is revered by others and is admired for his charisma and is regarded as a role model.

- Internal power, which means he has a great deal of confidence in his abilities as a businessman and has the self-esteem and self-belief to succeed.

As a top businessman, he is well aware of his reputation for being tough and powerful, and how others perceive him, which puts him in an automatic position of power. However, he is also acutely aware that although he could use his tough reputation to his advantage during negotiations, there is no point in abusing his position. So, before going into a negotiation, it is important to assess the balance of power. Amstrad may have been a huge success story with millions in the bank but, without their suppliers, they would have gone downhill fast. This is something that Sugar always kept in mind during negotiations with his suppliers.

Like all entrepreneurs, Sugar has exceptionally high expectations and knows exactly how to get what he wants.

During his Amstrad days, Sugar would, more often than not, enter negotiations with other parties that he already knew – his suppliers, for example. However, if he was approached by a new company that he had not heard of, he would make it his business to know everything there was to know about them before the meeting took place. As the manufacturing world was quite close-knit at the time, he was able to find out more about other companies by phoning his business associates and, usually, they would provide him with some inside information.

Sugar is also a big believer in face-to-face contact. Because more than 50% of our communication is transmitted through our body language, and the way in which we present ourselves, nothing beats face-to-face communication when negotiating a tricky deal. Although email is used prolifically these days for every form of communication, there is always a danger that messages can get lost or be misinterpreted – especially during a delicate negotiation. Meeting face to face is a much more personal and worthwhile way of communicating, and it helps to build relationships.

These days, the internet is such a valuable source of information that there is really no excuse for not doing homework in advance of a negotiation. Forewarned is forearmed, and nothing beats thorough research and hard facts when trying to agree terms.

USE YOUR NETWORK

One of the many reasons why Amstrad was so popular with the business community was because of Sugar's ability to make quick decisions. He was able to give answers and take action in a matter of days or, in some instances, hours. His word was enough to secure a deal and his business associates trusted that he would make good on all his promises. However, these days, it is difficult to be the only one calling the shots – even entrepreneurs need to call on the advice of their friends and colleagues when preparing for negotiating a deal.

Therefore, teamwork is very important when preparing a negotiation strategy. Brainstorming ideas and taking on different points of view help to cover all angles and ensure that you have all the answers to any difficult questions that may arise. Developing the most effective negotiation strategy takes time and patience but it requires lateral thinking. There may be only one main result that the team wants to achieve, but what happens if the other side refuses to comply? When both parties are trying to get their own way, there are bound to be potential sticking points that need to be worked through, and solutions created in advance of the negotiation.

Therefore, it is important to generate a number of options to turn to for each and every scenario. Sticking to a rigid Plan A will almost certainly end in a standstill; having a number of options to present to the other party shows that you are willing to be flexible and that you are keen to work out a deal. It is also important to have searching questions prepared when it looks like the negotiation is moving towards the dreaded deadlock. However, no matter what happens during the negotiation process, it is fundamentally important to always keep a close eye on the bottom line – never agree to anything that will turn out to be a loss-maker for your company.

Negotiating as a team means working together to achieve the optimum goal.

Companies such as Microsoft and Oracle are notoriously difficult to negotiate with, as they know everything there is to know about their products and are utterly certain that they are priced fairly. These are the toughest people to negotiate with, because they are full of confidence and self-belief, and are completely passionate about their product. So, if you plan to take on the likes of Microsoft, then it pays to be prepared!

It is fundamental to work as a team during the actual negotiation process. Each individual should know the role they are going to play and know exactly what they are going to say. It is also crucial not to jump in or talk over anyone else in the meeting. In Series 4 of *The Apprentice*, Claire and Alex demonstrated how not to carry out a negotiation when bidding for a rug in Morocco during one of the tasks. The team had agreed that Alex would negotiate with the shop owner, but when it came to it, Claire jumped in and her interruption cost the team £60 more than they would have paid in the first place.

Similarly, in *Sports Relief Does The Apprentice*, the politician Lembit Opik and comedian and presenter Hardeep Singh Kohli provided one of the most memorable moments of the celebrity *Apprentice* series so far. The task was to create a 'pop up' shop in London's West End, sell the stock and make as much money as possible. However, when it came to negotiating with the girls' team about choosing celebrity shop assistants, Lembit and Hardeep messed up terribly. Looking intimidated by the girls from the outset, Lembit nervously refused to continue the negotiation without consulting with the rest of his team. So, despite Hardeep's protestations, he actually left the room to talk to the team about how he should proceed. Needless to say, his team was less than impressed that he had walked out on the meeting, and had failed to make a decision on his own. Of course, the girls were thrilled, as Lembit's weakness at negotiating and lack of confidence was patently obvious, and they knew that the second he came back into the room, they would have the upper hand. It was no surprise that the girls won that round and continued on to win the entire competition, raising more than £400,000 for charity.

Sugar always honours a deal and can't stand those that renege on their promises.

Negotiating as a team means working together to achieve the optimum goal. A lack of team solidarity in a meeting looks unprofessional and is bound to end in disaster. Most importantly, never, ever walk out on a negotiation unless there is a logical reason for doing so or if both parties have agreed an adjournment. Gavin Kennedy, author of *Negotiation: An A–Z Guide* sums it up well when he says: 'Know when to talk and when to shut up; know when to say "maybe" and when to say "no"; know when to ask a question and what to answer when asked; and above all know when to prepare.'[2]

PATIENCE IS A VIRTUE

Negotiation is all about playing it cool and being patient. Rushing in or pressurizing the other side for an answer will not get you the results you want. Many of us yearn for instant gratification, but patience is actually regarded as a competitive advantage during the negotiation process. The ability to listen, empathize and remain mentally and physically relaxed are characteristics of a successful negotiator. Although Sugar might not come across as the most patient man, he knows how to play the waiting game when it comes to achieving his objectives.

Similarly, the global media mogul, Rupert Murdoch, a man not known for his ability to be easily won over, had nothing but praise for the ambitious Alan Sugar when he did a deal with Amstrad to manufacture satellite dishes in time for the launch of Sky Television in 1989. Again, Sugar impressed a notoriously hard-to-please businessman with his clear communication and his ability to make good on all his promises.

Although the deal between Murdoch and Sugar is now a success story, it took time and patience before a mutual agreement was worked out between Amstrad and Sky. In true Alan Sugar style, he had set about finding out how he could make the dishes for a low price. In the end, he found a metal-basher operation in Birmingham that churned out the metal part of the dish cheaply and in rapid succession. The dishes were eventually sold at £199 but had only cost £1 to make. Once again, Sugar had achieved an extremely impressive mark-up. It was this sort of initiative, together with his tremendous negotiating skills, that prompted Murdoch to announce at a press conference that Sugar was 'probably Britain's greatest entrepreneur'.

NURTURE RELATIONSHIPS

The most successful negotiations take place between two parties that have already enjoyed a long and fruitful relationship together. This means that before the negotiation process even begins a high level of trust and mutual respect already exists, which makes the process much easier.

For Sugar, one of the most important relationships he built up was with his suppliers. After all, Amstrad was dependent on its suppliers in order to get its products to the market. So Amstrad used the same suppliers for years – but that didn't mean that negotiation was out of the question. On the contrary, Sugar made a point of keeping them on their toes and often negotiated bigger and better deals that benefited both sides. During his Amstrad days, Sugar was a big believer in maintaining long-term relationships with his business partners, and did not switch to other suppliers lightly. If the competition were offering a better rate, then he would give his supplier the opportunity of coming up with an even more competitive proposition.

Sugar never adjusted his direct approach, even when he was dealing with the big boys from the City.

As a result, Amstrad's suppliers were tremendously loyal to Sugar and the boss would reward them with large-volume orders and repeat orders, should the product be successful. Another way that Sugar secured his relationship with his suppliers was by being honest with them at all times. He never made empty promises and always made sure that his word was followed through to the letter. However, when it came to ending a relationship with a supplier, he didn't shy away from telling them straight the reasons for his decision and being upfront and honest about the situation. In some cases, this approach actually served to strengthen the relationship. The supplier was incentivized to come up with a solution to the problem such as better service levels or better contract terms that mutually benefited both parties.

Building relationships depends on commitment from both sides. Sugar always honours a deal and can't stand those that renege on their promises. Even when mistakes are made, Sugar always stays with the deal, and never uses tricky business to get out of his commitments.

One of the ways that Sugar differentiated himself from his competitors was his ability to make quick and fast decisions.

This sense of loyalty and moral commitment to his business associates is far from his 'take-no-prisoners' image. While Sugar is no doubt a tough negotiator, he certainly treats his associates with respect and honesty. His style is more cooperative than coercive and he knows that using threats or making demands might get him the result in the short term, but will certainly not help him in the long term. There is no point in making enemies, particularly in the business world; people have long memories and will harbour resentment about how they were treated during the negotiation process. In fact, down the line, they might refuse to take part in any further discussions as a result. This sort of approach does not work in the business world when it comes to nurturing long-term relationships, so Sugar made sure that he always treated people fairly and with respect.

Sugar also made sure that he focused on the issue at hand rather than the people themselves. As he dealt with people from all walks of life, he knew, instinctively, how to behave and, crucially, how they would act in a tense negotiating situation. However, he never let his personal feelings about someone get in the way of the main topic, or let emotions run high. Even when discussions became heated, his business associates never took offence, as they knew his passion was directed towards solving the problem as opposed to delivering a personal attack. Once the meeting was over, all parties still remained on friendly terms and were able to have a good laugh about Sugar's fiery negotiation tactics.

Sugar never adjusted his direct approach, even when he was dealing with the big boys from the City. He thought nothing of dragging them from their plush offices in the central banking district in London to the less-than-salubrious Amstrad building in deepest darkest Essex. Meetings would be held in a shabby room full of boxes, with Sugar facing down the pristine suits from some of the world's most prestigious banking institutions. Although he had many adversaries from the City for many years, they seemed to admire him for his intelligence and his ability to stay true to himself.

Sugar's negotiation style was not designed to make enemies, but to outline his objectives, listen to what the other party had to say, and then figure out what made good business sense for both. Sugar was blessed with such a heightened sense of self-awareness that he knew exactly what buttons to press and how much he could get away with. His knowledge was so finely tuned and his logic was so sound, that even his biggest sceptics could not help but walk away from the negotiation table full of admiration and awe.

WRAP IT UP

So the preparation has been done, with goals and objectives clearly laid out, the team has been well-briefed, and the negotiation is going smoothly. Eventually, both parties reach a mutually satisfactory agreement and it is time to wrap things up. This can be one of the trickiest parts of negotiation, as it means getting the other party to commit to what has been decided in writing. There are many situations where a verbal agreement is reached, only for one of the parties to back out – so getting the client to sign on the dotted line is one way of ensuring that the deal is going to go ahead. Summarizing all the points of the meeting just before the end helps to clarify positions and is a way of reminding all parties about what has been agreed.

One of the ways that Sugar differentiated himself from his competitors was his ability to make quick and fast decisions. Once the deal was on the table, he would go through all the details, decide figures and go back and forth on certain points of the contract. As soon as everything had been ironed out, he would have contracts sent out immediately and have the whole deal signed and sealed in a matter of hours. Used to dealing with tons of paperwork and bureaucracy, his business associates would be surprised and impressed with Sugar's efficiency and ability to get things moving. However, it didn't end there. Sugar would make sure that he followed up on each of the terms of the agreement and monitored the other party and his own staff to make sure that both parties were keeping to their side of the bargain.

So just because the negotiation is over and terms have been agreed, it does not mean that there is no more work to be done.

Each side must fulfil their obligations and carry out all actions as written in the contract. Sugar is not a man to drop the ball or to let things slide, and his ability to keep an eye on his businesses on a regular basis is one of the many secrets of his success.

DRIVE A HARD BARGAIN

He may have a reputation for being a tough negotiator and he is certainly competitive, but it is his negotiating style that has earned Alan Sugar the respect of his many business associates. Straight-talking and to the point, Sugar doesn't mess around when there is a good deal on the table, but he also listens to the views of others and treats people fairly and with respect. He is a quick decision-maker and always comes through on his promises – qualities that have been essential in maintaining long-term business relationships.

- **Reach for the stars.** It is important to have a vision of what you want out of the negotiating process. Think big and set goals, but make sure you do enough preparation to prove to the other party that your goals make sense; otherwise they might not be convinced.
- **Use your network.** Sugar may have been top dog at Amstrad when it came to making the final decisions, but he always had friends and colleagues that he could consult with about certain parts of his negotiation strategy. No man is an island, so make sure you gather views from others and seek as much support as you can when preparing for negotiation.

- **Patience is a virtue.** Not all negotiations end in a deal; indeed, some can take months before an agreement has been reached. In these situations it is important to be patient and play the waiting game, rather than pressuring the other party into making a decision.
- **Nurture relationships.** Sugar is a fan of fostering long-term relationships. It is always easier to negotiate with people we already know, as a level of trust has already been built up. Therefore, nurturing relationships over time, following up on promises and being honest with each other can lead to successful agreements.
- **Wrap it up.** Following the summary of the negotiation process, and after verbal agreements have been exchanged, it is fundamental to get the terms signed and sealed. Sugar wastes no time in getting his business associates to sign on the dotted line and makes sure that they fulfil their contractual obligations.

7

INVEST IN THE RIGHT PEOPLE

'My staff tend to stay either 20 minutes or for 20 years!'[1]

– Alan Sugar

People are a company's most important asset and fundamental to the success and wealth of an organization. If people are treated like liabilities, they have the potential to bring down an entire company. Sick days, absenteeism and low morale can have a detrimental effect on productivity, which, in turn, has a knock-on effect on the firm's profits. Every time an employee leaves an organization and another one joins, there are significant associated costs. Similarly, companies spend massive amounts of money training employees and looking after their welfare. Therefore, it is vital that employers invest in the right people who will enhance the performance of their organization.

Although Sugar jokes that his main focus in business is making money, he also knows that his employees are his most valuable asset. Over the years, he has invested in people who he can trust, and has cultivated a loyal workforce and support network that he can always depend upon. So how did he do it? How did he know the right people to invest in?

As a young entrepreneur, he started hiring family members to help him with administrative tasks and other minor duties. He knew that he could trust his own family and people he already knew, but when the business started to expand, he realized he would have to venture out into the unknown and hire people that he had never met or heard of before. As an honest, determined, hardworking, high achiever himself, he naturally looked for those same qualities when choosing employees. He knew how valuable his staff was to helping him live out his dream, and wanted the best people working for him. It is a true testament to his own intuition that his Amstrad workforce remained strong, loyal and honest, and without them, he would never have achieved as much as he did. Finding the right kind of people to invest in is all about establishing the right fit for the company and its culture; the importance of this can never be underestimated.

Well known for his anti-bureaucracy stance, Sugar does not believe in formal management structures in his companies. Not one for micro-managing his staff, he sets the task and ensures it is delivered to his specifications. He also prefers not to pigeon-hole his staff into one skill-set; for example, an accountant could easily take on another role if he showed a talent in another area. He believes in giving his employees the leverage to grow and explore their different skills within a dynamic business environment, freedom rarely seen in the more formal management structures/hierarchies in most big firms today. However, allowing his employees to take on this level of responsibility requires a great degree of trust from both sides. This is why loyalty is one of Sugar's top requirements when hiring employees.

SURROUND YOURSELF WITH LOYAL STAFF

In 1987, Sugar gave a speech to students at City University Business School, and made the following tongue-in-cheek assertion:

> 'Pan Am takes good care of you. Marks and Spencer loves you. IBM says customer is king ... At Amstrad – we want your money.'[2]

It was very much Sugar's style to cut through the pretentiousness of other company slogans and show that Amstrad was a real organization that made no pretence about its main motivator: money. However, although Sugar was projected as a hard-nosed, money-orientated, cut-throat businessman, he was far removed from the one-dimensional character that he was purported to be. Of course money was a driving force for him, but he also valued the people that helped him make money and went to great lengths to ensure their wellbeing, encouraging them to take on new challenges, and rewarding them for their loyalty. It was this approach that encouraged employees to stay with Sugar for so many years, even when the going got really tough.

Today, loyalty is a quality that Sugar still values most in his employees and business associates. A staunchly loyal person himself, he expects the same treatment from others and never accepts being disappointed or let down. Two of Sugar's most recognizable colleagues over the years have been Nick Hewer and Margaret Mountford – his advisers on *The Apprentice*.

Well known for his anti-bureaucracy stance, Sugar does not believe in formal management structures in his companies.

An entrepreneur himself, Nick Hewer created his own PR company in the mid-1960s, where he represented a whole list of high profile clients including the secretariat of His Highness the Aga Khan. Nick first met Sugar in 1983 when his PR company was chosen to represent Amstrad. Heavily involved in Amstrad's business dealings, Nick became a loyal and trusted colleague and friend to Sugar, a friendship that has lasted almost 30 years.

Indeed, when Nick retired from the world of PR, Sugar arranged a dinner at The Dorchester in his honour. In a speech, Nick praised his good friend: 'Sir Alan is a very generous friend. The best thing about working for him was there was always something going on – he has vibrancy about him.' With one of the most recognizable faces in the UK, Nick is now a staple as an adviser on *The Apprentice*.

Similarly, Margaret Mountford has been one of Sugar's most trusted allies over the last 20 years. A City lawyer, Margaret first came in contact with Sugar when he decided to float Amstrad on the Stock Exchange. Other projects followed and a healthy friendship and mutual respect developed between the lawyer and the tycoon. Like Nick, Margaret has made quite an impression with her facial expressions and sharp wit on *The Apprentice*. However, unlike Nick, Margaret has retired from the show and will be replaced by Karren Brady, managing director of Birmingham City Football Club. Karren has already been featured on *The Apprentice* as an interviewer in the final episodes of each series.

Today, loyalty is a quality that Sugar still values most in his employees and business associates.

BEWARE OF THE PRETENDERS

Sugar invests in a certain type of person: someone who is loyal, honest, direct, trustworthy, quick on the uptake and makes decisions for the good of the company rather than for themselves. At first glance, it appears that Sugar invests in people that possess the exact same qualities as himself, and this is true, for the most part. However, despite his reputation for being the 'Delboy' of the business world, he does not favour or trust those that come across as aggressive, dishonest, or have a dubious sales patter and insincere gift of the gab. Every series of *The Apprentice* has its own motormouth, but when it comes to the final episodes, they are nowhere to be seen.

The perfectly groomed charmer Syed Ahmed, from Series 2 of *The Apprentice*, made all the right moves to impress Sugar – or so he thought. He talked a good game, won a few tasks and made some sales, but he lacked sincerity. In and outside the boardroom, he tried to convince anyone within hearing distance that he, like his hero, Alan Sugar, had also come from the school of hard knocks, and had struggled all his life to get what he wanted. By mirroring Sugar's behaviour and trying to 'chummy up' to him by claiming that he had exactly the same upbringing (they were both born in east London), it wasn't long before Sugar started to get fed up with Syed's very obvious strategy to get the boss on-side.

Syed's most unforgettable moment arrived in the form of his poor performance during one of the tasks where the teams had to make and sell food at the Thames Festival. It was Syed's idea to make fresh pizzas but he grossly miscalculated the number of chickens required to use as a pizza topping. Allocating one whole chicken per pizza, the team ended up with 100 chickens, thus blowing their budget and their credibility. In the boardroom, Syed was in the firing line as he was the one that had insisted on ordering that many chickens – but although he ended up being at the brunt of one of Sugar's angriest tirades of the series, he still managed to escape being fired. However, a few weeks later, his number finally came up. Sugar found it difficult to pin him down on anything. His unwillingness to take responsibility for making a mistake in the interests of self-preservation was too much for the tycoon to bear. Syed's lack of sincerity and accountability together with an indifferent eye for detail meant he was given his marching orders and sent home.

Hailed as Britain's 'most belligerent boss', Sugar has a reputation for being short-tempered and impatient.

Despite his consistent attempts to persuade Sugar that he was a sure-fire candidate for the prize, it is clear that even if Syed Ahmed had won, he would not have fitted into the company culture that Sugar has carefully cultivated in his different organizations over the last 40 years. Nor would he have lasted too long. The problem with hiring charmers is their ability to antagonize others. They may be charismatic and gifted at making presentations or coming up with the odd idea, but they can also appear insincere and slow to admit to making mistakes. These are the sorts of elements of Syed's character that irritated his fellow apprentices, Sugar himself and pretty much most of the nation. While charmers are undoubtedly great television, putting Syed among hardworking, direct, ambitious, upfront teamworkers would have not been a decision that Sugar would have been proud of.

STAY CLEAR OF THE TEMPER TANTRUMS

Hailed as Britain's 'most belligerent boss', Sugar has a reputation for being short-tempered and impatient. However, he has also confessed that he has mellowed with age and has far more tolerance than he used to. But just because Sugar had a bit of a temper in his younger days does not mean that he admires hot-headedness in others. Of course, he will put up with a bit of cheek and is clearly amused by some of the outrageous behaviour displayed by the more passionate apprentices that have crossed his path, but that does not encourage him to award the fiery character with a £100,000-a-year job in one of his companies.

Probably the fieriest character on *The Apprentice* to date is Paul Torrisi from Series 1. On the positive side, he was bright, ambitious and charismatic, and he had an uncanny talent for striking up conversations with random people in order to make sales. His sales patter was peppered with personal information, whether it was true or not, to ensure that he found some common ground with his prospective client; for example, if he spotted an accent, he would guess that person's nationality, and if he was right, he would claim that his mother or aunt or uncle was from the same country – a useful technique for getting people onside.

'There's only room for one big mouth in my organization, and that's me.'

However, in spite of his obvious skill as a salesman and his drive to succeed, he was brought into the boardroom by his team mates time and time again. Although he was usually the hardest working on each task, he was unpopular with his fellow contestants because of his fiery temper. When he wasn't the team leader, he could not accept someone else giving the orders and clashed constantly with the others, especially his teammate Saira Khan. Slammed by Nick Hewer for being 'sexist beyond belief', Paul Torrisi appeared to have a problem with women who were in a position of authority, and was not shy about airing his views on the subject.

Paul's lowest point was during the art task, where both teams were challenged to sell expensive art to prospective buyers. With no knowledge of art at all and dismissive of the task from the beginning, it was not surprising that he did not excel in this task. In the end, it was ego and his inability to reign in his temper that led Sugar to dismiss him from the competition.

Again, the Paul Torrisis of this world are born entertainers and make great television, but they do not make the best employees. Throwing temper tantrums in the middle of an office environment shows a lack of professionalism and sets a bad example for other members of staff.

TRUST YOUR INTUITION

Making the right hiring choices always comes down to intuition. You may not be able to put your finger on why you feel someone would be better suited to your company culture over someone else, but going with your gut instinct is sure to help you make the right investment. As one self-made entrepreneur says:

> 'When you are starting a business on your own, money is always tight, but when the business expands you have no choice but to hire staff to grow the company. However, you also need to work out the financial implications: what will their annual salary be? Are you going to give them paid holidays or pay them for overtime? Will you offer paid sick leave? Going from a one-man operation to a team environment is a huge mental and financial leap. Therefore, it is crucial to use your instincts and invest in the right people to make sure that the transition is as smooth as possible. This involves making careful staffing decisions and taking time to choose the right people for the company culture you are trying to create.'

When Sugar chose Yasmina Siadatan over the serious contender, Kate Walsh, to be his fifth apprentice, he said on *The Apprentice: You're Hired*: 'My instincts are telling me that Yasmina's the right one for the job.' Sugar has made most of the decisions in his life based on his keen sense of intuition. He is interested in how people operate and likes to study body language and the way others express themselves. With an uncanny gift for getting the measure of people within a split second, he knows exactly who to trust with a job.

However, hiring Yasmina was not just about gut instinct; otherwise he would have hired her in the first episode. Yasmina proved herself over the course of the 12 weeks to be efficient and hardworking, and although she made mistakes, she took responsibility for them. Hiring Yasmina over the extremely capable pitch-perfect Kate Walsh caused a bit of controversy but, in the end, it comes down to the best person for the role and who is the best fit for the organization.

DON'T HIRE PEOPLE EXACTLY LIKE YOURSELF

When investing in people, it is tempting to hire those with the same skillset and qualities as ourselves. Certainly, Alan Sugar likes to hire people that seem to emulate his tough work ethic. However, that does not mean that he necessarily looks for people who possess the same characteristics as him – as he says, often enough, 'there's only room for one big mouth in my organization, and that's me'.

Ruth Badger from Series 2 was probably the closest in personality to Sugar. She was driven, hardworking, forceful, opinionated and assertive; she excelled at sales and fought her corner like a tigress in the boardroom. She impressed the boss and his two sidekicks time and again with her leadership skills and ability to win task after task. It seemed obvious that 'The Badger', as she came to be known, would run away with the title of The Apprentice. However, in the end, Ruth was a very worthy runner-up to the quietly spoken 'silent assassin' Michelle Dewberry, and exited the competition.

So, why didn't Ruth get the job? Even Margaret Mountford said that Ruth 'should have won', but Sugar didn't agree. Although Ruth was undoubtedly a workhorse, and got results, she probably would have clashed with the boss himself if she had become his apprentice. The key to making the right investment in people is to take stock of your own skills and hire people to complement them rather than matching them exactly. Strong personalities are important to have in any organization, but there can only be so many of them. There is a good chance that with their similarities and strong opinions, Sugar would have clashed quite heavily with his new apprentice. It is clear that Ruth is a woman of strong opinions and not a person that would be easily moulded. This would have caused tension between her and her new boss.

> **The key to making the right investment in people is to take stock of your own skills and hire people to complement them rather than matching them exactly.**

Simon Ambrose from Series 3 became Sugar's next apprentice, beating the clear favourite Kristina Grimes. Grimes had been so impressive during all the tasks that many believed she was a shoe-in for the role. But if we think about what being an apprentice really means, then it is understandable why Ambrose was probably the better choice. With her extensive experience and forthright manner, Grimes is more of a leader than a follower and, like Ruth Badger, would probably have clashed with Sugar in the workplace. Not known for his leadership skills, Ambrose is more relaxed in his attitude and willing to follow orders without too much questioning; he even said that if Sugar gave him 'a tea-making job' he would do it. Whether Ambrose has had to make tea is not known, but unlike some other past apprentices, he has proved he can go the distance. Two years on from his victory, Ambrose is still working for Sugar at his real estate company, Amsprop.

Whereas seemingly the most suitable candidate is someone similar to the boss, it pays to bear in mind that too many chiefs in an organization can lead to disharmony and a fractious working culture.

INVEST IN THE RIGHT PEOPLE

The importance of people in relation to the success of an organization can never be underestimated. Investing in the right sort of staff is a skill in itself and takes time, intuition and careful consideration. Choosing the wrong employee can have serious ramifications for an organization and can prove to be a costly mistake. Sugar chooses his apprentices based not only on his gut instinct but through their ability to prove themselves as being worthy contenders for the six-figure salary. Week after week, he weeds out the pretenders, the charmers, the motormouths and the manipulators, until he arrives at his final decision in week 12. For the most part, his apprentices have proved to be assets to his various companies and have remained loyal to their boss.

- **Surround yourself with loyal staff.** Some of Sugar's first employees were his family and close friends because he knew that he could trust them. Building up a loyal support network is vital in business and it is a testament to Sugar's skill as a manager that many of his staff have stayed with him for so many years.

- **Beware of the pretenders.** There are many potential employees who can talk their way out of any situation and refuse to take responsibility for their mistakes. There have been quite a few 'pretenders' on *The Apprentice* – although they provided some of television's most memorable moments, they never got the job because there is often not much substance behind all the charm and bluster.
- **Stay clear of the temper tantrums.** Although Sugar is known to have a short fuse, it doesn't mean that he wants to invest in someone that has a problem controlling their temper in the workplace. A fiery character might get some results but it is usually at the expense of someone else, and can easily serve to alienate the entire team.
- **Trust your intuition.** Intuition, gut instinct or hunch – whatever you want to call it – it helps us to make decisions. Although Sugar credits his 'gut' for making tough business decisions, he does not just use intuition alone, but seeks the advice of others and does his homework before deciding on his plan of action.
- **Don't hire people exactly like yourself.** Hiring people is about adding to your own skillset rather than duplicating it. Sugar looks for potential candidates who follow the same work ethic as himself, but are not so aggressive or opinionated that they would clash with the boss, himself, or the rest of the office team.

8

LEAD FROM THE FRONT

'A leader has two important characteristics: first, he is going somewhere; second, he is able to persuade other people to go with him.'

– Maximilien Francois Robespierre

The subject of leadership has been heavily debated by philosophers, politicians, heads of organizations, business gurus, military leaders and sports coaches. Although there are many theories out there about what makes a good leader, there are certain qualities an individual must possess in order to lead a team. Alan Sugar embraces all of them: charisma, vision, integrity, courage, confidence, passion, perseverance, character, a willingness to take risks and the ability to inspire and motivate others.

Alan Sugar believes that leaders are born, not made, but does concede that it is possible to make the transition into a leadership role a bit later on in life. However, in Sugar's case, it is clear that he is a born leader who was always meant to be at the helm, steering his team to success. His leadership skills have even been recognized by the government: in 2007, he was invited to join Gordon Brown's business leaders' council, alongside other esteemed businessmen such as Tesco and BP chief executives Terry Leahy and Tony Heywood. Their role was to offer advice and share their extensive experience with regard to business and economic issues.

LEAD AND NURTURE

It is true that leaders should embody the same qualities that they expect from their employees, but they must also stand out from the crowd. Alan Sugar's tough but fair attitude, together with a keen sense of humour, has won him a great deal of admiration both inside and outside the business world.

So, how do we define leadership? Philip Whiteley is an author and journalist who specializes in management, particularly in the areas of leadership, motivation and strategic human resources. His most recent publication is *Meet the New Boss*, which looks at how culture has shaped the way we view management and the workplace. He says:

> 'I think that there is too much of a tendency to think that leaders are mostly one thing or another: e.g., are they nice or nasty, charismatic or introverted? This is a simplistic way of thinking about leadership. Leaders are human beings, not just a collection of two or three competences.

> 'The public image of Alan Sugar is that he's tough, and of Richard Branson that he's nice, but I'm sure that the attributes of both are much more multi-faceted than that. My interviews with leaders over the past ten years indicate that the best are able to be nurturing and ruthless simultaneously. This sounds like a contradiction, but it's not. It is, however, a paradox, and people who are comfortable with paradox and ambiguity are better able to become leaders than those who prefer cast-iron certainties and linear thinking. The best leaders are nurturing to your key talent and the communication and morale of key teams, both while and by making tough decisions on costs and prioritization of activities. They don't let matters drift; they deal with poor performance, and they are hugely motivational to those who do perform and want to perform. Once it's broken down in this way, the paradox becomes understandable and you realize that it isn't a contradiction.'

Sugar's leadership style is not based on being the most popular or the most well-liked. He admits he can be tough at times, and that he has extremely high expectations. Part of being a leader is the ability to make tough decisions, and these might not always win him favour with everybody. Indeed, the real test of a good leader is to see how he reacts in a crisis. As Theodore Roosevelt said, 'In any moment of

Alan Sugar believes that leaders are born, not made.

decision, the best thing you can do is the right thing, the next best thing is the wrong thing, and the worst thing you can do is nothing'. It is hard to please people all of the time, but good leaders have the integrity to stand by their decisions and usually weather the brief storm of unpopularity; after all, every decision they make is for the good of the company.

Furthermore, if the leader involves his staff in the decision-making process, then they understand the reasons why a certain decision is being made, and are far more forgiving as a result. John Adair, one of the world's leading authorities on leadership and leadership development, believes that 'everyone in the company – employees and shareholders – should share in the rewards of success and the consequences of failure'.[1]

Sugar has always managed to win the respect and loyalty of his followers by setting a good example. He values honesty and has an inclusive management style that appeals to his staff. Although he may have the reputation of being a tough taskmaster, he always makes sure that hard work, relentless effort and honesty are handsomely rewarded.

ENGAGE WITH YOUR STAFF

One of the ways that Sugar led Amstrad was by creating an informal, flexible company structure that did away with red tape and petty bureaucracy. He had no time for hours and hours of meetings ever day, something that is so common to corporations today. Endlessly analyzing and planning was not his style; he was a man of action and had no problem letting everybody know it.

There was no need for clients to go through layers of management in order to get a decision; at Amstrad the doors were always very much open and a transparency existed in the company that was unique and appealing at the time. Because there was no real hierarchy, everybody was treated as an equal and allowed to make important decisions. They even had a chance to make their case to the boss himself; in a business world where most leaders of the top organizations so rarely make an appearance that they seem like fantasy figures, pitching an idea to the top man himself was truly an exciting (if nerve-wracking) prospect to most Amstrad staff. Yet no matter what level the employee operated, Sugar would always give them a fair hearing.

Sugar's employees may have grumbled now and then, but they still worked hard to please him – because praise from Alan Sugar is praise indeed.

Malcolm Miller, who spent 16 years working alongside Sugar at Amstrad, described how employees would be given the opportunity to pitch their ideas to the big boss. Miller would encourage them to go and present their ideas to Sugar, who would listen carefully before expressing his thoughts on the subject. Straight-talking was the name of the game, and Sugar did not spare anyone's feelings when it came to airing his views, but that was the Amstrad way. As Miller said: 'If you don't like straight talking or you're shocked by being told your idea is crap, then don't come to Amstrad, because we don't pull our punches.'[2]

He may be direct but at least everyone knows where they stand at the end of it.

This is very much the style that Sugar adopts in *The Apprentice*. He listens to people, thinks about what they have said, and then tells them why their idea will or will not work. He may be direct but at least everyone knows where they stand at the end of it; they learn from the experience and either go away exhilarated that their idea has been accepted by the notoriously hard-to-please businessman, or disappointed that they have failed to please him – but also determined to impress him on their next task.

A good leader always listens to his staff, irrespective of what role they play or the level they are at. Sugar's inclusive business style has earned him the respect and loyalty of his employees. They might have grumbled now and then, but they still worked hard to please him – because praise from Alan Sugar is praise indeed.

Good leaders may be passionate visionaries who have the talent of persuasion and the ability to inspire others, but they always keep a very close eye on the bottom line. While focusing on motivating staff and allowing them the freedom to grow and develop is a worthy pursuit, the organization would not be a success if there was not also a strong focus on the facts and figures. Sugar has continually emphasized the importance of being bottom-line orientated.

Staff are fundamental to the success of an organization but they won't hang around long if they are not being paid. Part of a leader's responsibilities is to ensure the financial welfare of the staff, and this involves paying close attention to the numbers. Sugar has always thrived on facts and figures and is completely committed to achieving the best financial results. He also makes sure that he communicates the bottom-line objectives to his staff so they can play a part in working towards these goals. By giving his employees clarity of purpose, they feel more engaged with the task at hand and have more of a sense of pride – especially when they achieve their bottom-line objectives, knowing that they were instrumental in acquiring the result.

So passion, and the ability to inspire and motivate, helps to get others on board when striving to reach a common goal. But staff must be included in exactly what the company is trying to achieve and the roles they need to play in order to succeed – an approach that Sugar has advocated throughout his career.

LEAD BY EXAMPLE

Every great leader has a vision. From the moment he started boiling beetroot for the greengrocers or selling home-made ginger beer to his school friends, Sugar knew what he wanted to do in life. He wanted to sell and he wanted to be the best he could be at it. This is one of the most important traits of a good leader: to know what you want to achieve. If you don't have a clear vision about what direction you want the business to take, others will not know either. Therefore, Alan Sugar has always understood the value of direct communication to ensure that others are acutely aware of the company's goals and that they share in his vision.

Similarly, he never dictated to people. Certainly, he told them what he wanted done, and when they had to deliver – but he never told them how they should do it. He wasn't interested in micro-managing the Amstrad staff; if he assigned them a task, he expected them to get on with it and come up with a result by a certain deadline. How they went about the task was entirely up to them. If the team was encountering problems then he offered guidance and support where necessary but, overall, he fully believed in giving his staff the responsibility and autonomy to decide on how a project should be tackled. In fact, he encouraged his staff to be creative and innovative where possible. As George S. Patton once said, 'Never tell people how to do things. Tell them what to do and they will surprise you with their ingenuity.'

'Never tell people how to do things. Tell them what to do and they will surprise you with their ingenuity.'

Similarly, he always made sure, when delegating, that he played to people's strengths. This is a mistake that Helene Speight made when leading her team in a task during Series 4 of *The Apprentice*. The task was to go to a major shopping centre and persuade shoppers to get their photos taken. One of the team members, Lucinda Ledgerwood, was very upfront about her lack of technical prowess and explained to her team leader that she 'was useless with computers' and 'can't even use a mobile phone'. Instead of assigning Lucinda a task that would play to her strengths, Helene gave her the job of downloading and editing the photos, which, of course, resulted in disaster, and a fiery exchange between the two women. With such dissension in the ranks, the team failed the task.

People will always respect a leader who works even harder than them. In the 1980s, there was a culture where top bosses were more often seen 'networking' on the golf courses or dining out in fancy restaurants, talking business over five-hour lunches.

Alan Sugar made a point of being in the office every day, suggesting that he is very much against this type of behaviour. When staff see the boss on-site every day, working tirelessly to achieve a goal, they can't help but respect their leader and follow his example.

Sugar created a working culture where everybody was equal and although he was the boss, he never gave himself special favours or lorded his success over his 'subordinates'. Unlike his City contemporaries, he didn't have an office, preferring to sit out on the floor with the rest of his employees. Yes, he was the boss, but he never made any pretensions about how he had risen up the ranks: he was a working class grafter and proud of it. Even when he became wealthy beyond imagination, he lived a pretty modest lifestyle for someone of his standing. He bought himself a nice house in Essex and treated himself to the infamous Rolls-Royce but, comparatively speaking, he certainly didn't live the lifestyle of the rich and famous, nor did he flaunt his wealth.

With his knighthood and plethora of business awards, it seems that Alan Sugar has every right to allow himself a few airs and graces, but he still remains the same old feisty character from the East End. To his staff and his work colleagues, he is the same honest, hardworking man as he has always been, and they can't help but respect him for it. He may be demanding, but he has the right to make his demands because nobody sets a better example for hard work than he does.

LEADING A HORSE TO WATER

As Dwight D. Eisenhower famously said, 'You do not lead by hitting people over the head – that's assault, not leadership.' One of the biggest mistakes that leaders make is to dictate to people. Throughout history, there have been countries run by dictatorships but this kind of leadership has never ended well. Treating people ruthlessly and mercilessly is not the best way to win their loyalty and respect. In fact, it builds resentment and bitterness.

Although he is sometimes tough and demanding, Sugar also listens carefully to the suggestions of others, and clearly gives his reasons why he doesn't like something. A good leader will not be popular all of the time but people will always respect someone who listens and provides constructive feedback. Sugar does come across as a bit scary and his colleagues have verified this point, but many would argue that fear is a great motivator. It is usually the teacher we are most frightened of at school that we work the hardest for, and it is praise from that teacher that gives us a sense of pride. However, people do not respond to fear alone but nor do we expect all our needs to be satisfied. If the boss is demanding, then he must be clear about why he is putting pressure on his staff to carry out a certain task, and what it means for the company. In turn, the employees must be allowed to ask questions and clarify the nature of the task. Again, it is his inclusive style and his ability to put his ego aside that makes Sugar an exemplary leader.

There is no room for an ego among leaders. One ex-banker described how a company he worked for fell apart before his very eyes, all because of the egos of the managers and chief executives:

> '*I worked as an accountant and frequently reported to the heads of the different departments. Although they worked for the same organization, they refused to listen to each other and begrudged anyone that came up with*

a suggestion that they perceived as better than theirs. They guarded information fiercely and didn't like that I shared my data with the different heads. Employees in 'less important' positions were known as 'the underlings' and suggestions made by them were immediately dismissed. Of course, in the end, nothing got done and the 'leaders' were so wrapped up in their internal politics that they took their eye off the ball, stopped paying attention to the economy, and failed to respond to market changes. About three months after I left, the company went bankrupt – hardly surprising, really.'

Sugar left his ego at the door as soon as he started to build his own company. He knew that patronizing or looking down on people would win him no favours. His open-door policy meant that staff saw him as approachable and willing to listen to their suggestions. Creating a level playing field is one of the most important activities for a leader if he wants the respect of his staff, irrespective of the hierarchy of an organization.

However, during *The Apprentice* tasks, not every project leader has adopted the 'all men are created equal' approach. The teams are generally split into two with each team headed up by a project manager. The purpose of the project manager is to lead the team to victory through the use of good leadership skills. Leaders that shout, dictate or assume an air of superiority and arrogance will not get the response they are looking for from their team. This is a lesson that Rory Laing from Series 3 of *The Apprentice* learned the hard way.

The task was to design a dog accessory. From the outset, it appeared that Rory was so excited to be leader for the day that he let the power go completely to his head. In a brainstorming session, he began to lay down the law in an autocratic way, speaking to his 'underlings' as if they were naughty schoolboys. He dictated his own terms to them, without allowing them to respond and steamrolled ahead with his idea for a 'pooch pouch', a utility belt for dog walkers that was a cumbersome, unattractive device, which would have little appeal to the target market. A major personality clash with the strong-willed, fiery Tre Azam did nothing to raise his profile in the eyes of the team. During one argument, he continually insisted to Tre, 'I am your boss', to which Tre replied, 'You're nothing to me'.

If you have to lay down the law and keep reminding people that you are the boss, then you don't really believe it yourself.

As leader, Rory had failed to exhibit any of the leadership skills necessary to ensure respect and loyalty from the team. He was patronizing, dictatorial, controlling and arrogant, and spoke down to his team members as if he had forgotten that they were all on the same side, reaching for a common goal. Of course, the team failed the task and Rory was given his marching orders, with Sugar pronouncing him 'a disaster'. The lesson here is that if you have to lay down the law and keep reminding people that you are the boss, then you don't really believe it yourself. Rory showed his weaknesses as a leader too soon, and from the minute they sat down to brainstorm, it was clear that the task was already doomed.

THE TRUTH ALWAYS WINS

A good leader is ethical and always honest, even in the most uncomfortable situations. It is very difficult to argue with the truth, and a leader must have sound principles in order to win the respect of his contemporaries. When Amstrad went through its 'year of disaster', City analysts were very impressed by how forthright Sugar was about the mistakes he had made. He never assigned blame, accused market conditions for the fall in profits, or attempted to cover himself by making up excuses. Instead – and against the advice of his PR staff – he insisted in calling Amstrad's darker days as a 'disaster' and refused to put any kind of spin on what had happened. This approach won him a lot of praise from the media, as well as from the City and really proved what an excellent leader he was.

There is no such thing as the 'right' type of leadership style. It depends on the individual and the type of character they have. However, if a leader expects to have his demands met time and again, then he must have consistency of character. Alan Sugar is nothing if not consistent. He is straight-down-the-line and always lets people know where they stand. It is not to say that he is predictable, but anyone that has ever worked with him will know that he doesn't tolerate laziness, deceit or a failure to take accountability. He can't stand yes-men, and enjoys being challenged by his colleagues. He admits that he has a temper, but he has learned to control his anger. With one look, he can let you know exactly how things should be, and that is a powerful skill to possess. To get on this leader's best side, it is wise to be honest, ethical and hardworking, otherwise you will get short shrift.

Although consistency of character is a valuable thing, leaders must also be willing to embrace change. Competition is fiercer than ever in a global economy and leaders must always watch the markets and respond faster than anyone else. During his Amstrad days, Sugar had an almost uncanny ability to predict changes in the market. He instinctively knew what the customer wanted and he would move heaven and earth to provide them with it. The root of his success was his ability to embrace change. Although he no longer runs Amstrad, he still applies this rule of flexibility to his other ventures, with outstanding results.

It is clear that Alan Sugar is a born leader. He embraces all the qualities of a natural leader, and it is clear that he could never work for anyone else. Alan Sugar was born to lead, never to follow.

LEAD FROM THE FRONT

Alan Sugar is a born leader who has the inbuilt talent and qualities to inspire and motivate others. He is tough but fair, and believes in giving praise when it is due. His leadership style is inclusive; he does not create class boundaries or dismiss those who operate in 'lower' level roles. A good listener and speaker, Sugar treats his employees with respect, and they have remained loyal and committed to their leader as a result.

- **Lead and nurture.** Sugar's leadership style focuses on getting the best out of people. He is not concerned about being the most popular boss in the world, but works hard to earn the respect and loyalty from his employees and contemporaries.
- **Engage with your staff.** Sugar makes a point of directly contributing to the projects at hand. He sets the task but always communicates well and listens to questions and suggestions from others. His unconventional management structure is based on fairness and a level playing field, and he welcomes all opinions.

- **Lead by example.** Every leader must set a good example for his staff. One of the ways to get employees on board with an idea is to have them share in the vision. Sugar always made sure that his employees knew exactly where the company was going and the benefits they would receive if goals were successfully attained.

- **Leading a horse to water.** As the old expression goes, 'You can lead a horse to water but you can't make it drink'. A dictatorial leader will never win any long-term respect or loyalty from his followers. Similarly, there is no space for a giant ego when guiding a team; it only builds bitterness and resentment.

- **The truth always wins.** Sugar has always advocated truth and honesty – two of a leader's most important qualities. He has never swayed from this approach and has always been very upfront about the mistakes he has made. People will always respect a leader for their willingness to accept accountability; it shows strength of character and increases their likeability.

9

WIN AS A TEAM

'Coming together is a beginning. Keeping together is progress. Working together is success.'

– Henry Ford

When it comes to business, it is easy to regard Sugar as a maverick: someone who comes up with original ideas, takes risks and makes big decisions. However, a good maverick does not work alone; every maverick needs a good team behind him in order to make his entrepreneurial dreams a reality.

Sugar may have operated on his own at the beginning of his career, but as he built up his business, he realized the importance of cultivating a team of loyal supporters. Not only did he lead his team to success, but he was also part of the team, helping them to carry out actions and assignments, and where necessary giving them direction. As Sugar says, 'Without the help and support of other people, not only among their own team, but also in partnership with other businesses and business advisers, a business loner will not survive.'[1]

The combined talents of his results-focused team of employees and business associates ensure continued success for Sugar and his current ventures.

Douglas Miller, author of *Brilliant Teams*, believes:

> *'What* The Apprentice *shows us is that those who can reconcile their own ambitions with the recognition that these ambitions can only be achieved through and with the help of others, are the ones who are most likely to win. The camera, in this case the moving camera, never lies. Those who lack the ability or more importantly, the desire to form relationships with other potential apprentices, soon get exposed. "People users" lose self-control, argue and often reveal aggressive behaviour (mistakenly believing that this is what being 'tough' in business is about) when they cannot carry a group of people with them. 'Relationship builders' know that, even though it can be difficult, the route to*

personal success lies in their ability to pull a potentially disparate group with conflicting personal agendas together in a particular direction.

'So what do we learn from The Apprentice? *That you cannot succeed alone. That your personal goals can only be met through cooperation and collaboration with others. That the manifestation of this collaborative approach is the creation of a dynamic group of people who share similar aspirations. In the world of work we call this a "team". Teams are the backbone of business success and without them we fail individually and collectively.'*

In *The Apprentice*, the contestants are usually entrepreneurial types, used to getting their own way; their challenge is to work as part of a team without letting their egos trip them up. The 'natural leaders' quickly find out that they will not succeed by alienating their teams, and these are usually the ones that end up, eventually, getting fired. There is no space for egos in a team. A good team realizes that they can only deliver a task by working together.

WORK AS A TEAM

'Not finance. Not strategy. Not technology. It is teamwork that remains the ultimate competitive advantage, both because it is so powerful and so rare.'[2]

Patrick Lencioni

Communication is key to any team's success and it is vital that each team member is included in each stage of the process. When it comes to preparing a pitch, the team must be aware of what is going to be said and how the pitch is going to be approached.

Even if there is only one person presenting the product or service to prospective clients, it is still important that the rest of team knows exactly how that person is going to approach the topic.

Rachel Groves from Series 1 of *The Apprentice* took everyone by surprise when she threw off her shoes during a pitch and started dancing, with abandon, to Amstrad's new Jukebox music system. It was clear from the expressions on her team-mates' faces that they had not been briefed about Rachel's plan to, spontaneously, display this act of *joie de vivre*. Similarly, the prospective clients looked amused and mortified at the same time. Rachel's approach, together with a poor advertising campaign, saw the team failing miserably. In the boardroom, it was obvious whose neck was on the chopping block this time; Sugar made no bones about who was next to be fired, and Rachel was removed from the competition.

Creativity and innovation are qualities that are to be applauded in a team environment. After all, it is original thinking that got Sugar to the position he is in today. However, if you are planning on taking a more 'original' approach, then make sure you run the idea past your team or at least keep them informed about what you are planning to do. Perhaps if Rachel had told her team about what she planned to do during her pitch, they would have advised her otherwise and the whole sorry incident need not have happened at all.

CULTIVATE RESPECT AND LOYALTY

Former military man Paul Callaghan, from Series 3, created one of the most memorable tasks from *The Apprentice* so far. The task was to choose a home-grown British product and try to sell it abroad in a French market. Callaghan, the team leader, decided that cheap blocks of cheddar from a cash-and-carry and some pork sausages would certainly appeal to his target consumers. Given that France is known for its superior cheese, Callaghan could not have made a worse decision. His team-mates aired their doubts, but their leader did not listen and set about buying all the stock in preparation for the task ahead.

When the question arose about how they were to cook sausages on a market stall, Callaghan came up with the perfect plan. He devised a cooking implement that comprised of an empty tin of baked beans, placed on a burner, topped with a frying pan. Not one of the team-members was particularly shocked when the sausages failed to cook properly. In the end, it was clear that Callaghan had lost the respect of his team-mates and they had given up on him

There is no space for egos in a team. A good team realizes that they can only deliver a task by working together.

and the task. In fact, they appeared to be in a 'give him enough rope and he'll hang himself' sort of mode, which is, of course, precisely what happened. The team ended up making a significant loss, which frustrated Sugar, and it was *au revoir* to Callaghan.

On the other hand, the rival team had a better strategy and picked English teas, jams and smoked fish to market to their French customers. Although It is difficult to promote tea in a coffee-drinking nation, their choice of product was far superior to the other team and, unsurprisingly, they emerged victorious.

Once the loyalty and support of the team has gone, the task will almost certainly end in failure. Callaghan should have made more effort to listen to his team-mates' doubts about selling cheese to the French, but, similarly, his team-mates should have made more of an effort to put their point across. Of course, *The Apprentice* is a competition and as such involves a certain amount of ruthlessness – but the team gave up on Callaghan and the task quite quickly, knowing that his cards were marked the second he chose the wrong product. Perhaps, if they had come together to create a better strategy then they would have won and there would have been no need to prey on the weaknesses of the team leader.

PUT ASIDE PERSONAL DIFFERENCES

One of the major functions of a successful team is the ability to inspire and motivate each other. Team members are not necessarily motivated by money alone, and want to be regarded as an important part of the team and feel that their individual role has had some influence on the outcome of the task. Content team members thrive off a sense of achievement and feel personal fulfilment when they contribute to the success of the team. A good team leader will encourage and motivate their team, rewarding them with increased responsibility and providing them with opportunities to progress in their careers.

A team is only as strong as its members, and there is no room for the 'weakest link' in a chain of command. When a team is assigned a project, all of the members must embrace the task and do their best with what they have been instructed to do. It is important during the planning process that opinions are shared and points exchanged, but the main thing is that everybody is on board with the task at hand.

In *The Apprentice*, there is rivalry within the teams as well as between the teams. This is not so dissimilar to a real working environment where team members try to out-do each other in order to be seen to shine the brightest. Competition is healthy within a team, because it motivates and challenges its members, but attempting in any way to bring down a team-mate through negativity or manipulation is not the sign of a good team player. Similarly, team-mates that voice disapproval or use the benefit of hindsight to prove that they are right do not make themselves particularly popular. One marketing executive remembers one person on his team who loved to disagree with every decision the team made, and then crowed with delight when things went awry:

> 'As you can imagine, this voice of dissent was not at all popular in our team. As a marketing team, our role was to come up with creative ways to market our products to our target consumer.

> 'As soon as we started mapping out our marketing strategy, a voice would pipe up from the back of the room, telling us that the idea would never work, but not really explaining why. It was like he was disagreeing with the rest of the team just for the sake of it. Obviously in a group situation, you expect to receive differing opinions, and feedback is, of course, crucial to the ideas process.

> 'However, this person constantly rubbished all our suggestions without coming up with any ideas of his own. Then if higher management rejected our strategy, he would nod his head smugly as if he knew all along that this would happen. Our team ended up nicknaming him The King of Hindsight or The Man with the Crystal Ball.'

Although the self-confessed 'intuitive' Lorraine Tighe from Series 5 did well in *The Apprentice*, reaching the all-important interview stage at week 11, she caused tension in the team because of her unwillingness to fully engage in the tasks. Hailed as the 'Cassandra' of the show by Margaret Mountford, Lorraine was simply never listened to by her team-mates and her instincts usually ended up being right.

Of course, her team-mates should have treated her with more respect and given her a platform to air her views, but perhaps Lorraine could have been a little more forceful in expressing her opinions during the planning stage of each task. However, when a whole team has agreed on a path, it is better to push all other negative feelings aside and get involved, rather than shouting disapproval and making judgements from the sidelines. After all, a team that fully engages in a shared goal will always have a better chance of achieving the desired result. Lorraine had a habit of using the benefit of hindsight to cast aspersions on an already completed task, which only served to upset and irritate her team-mates.

Communication is key to any team's success and it is vital that each team member is included in each stage of the process.

Negativity is one of the most dangerous attitudes that can filter into a team, and can have a detrimental impact on the team's success. There is nothing wrong with voicing concerns as long as these opinions are constructive. Saying that something 'won't work', without following up with suggestions as to how to overcome the problem will only cause bad feeling in the team. However, refusing to take part or 'sulking' because people have not seen things your way is a sign of a big ego, which is not acceptable in a team environment.

Similarly, Lucinda Ledgerwood from Series 4 took up the role as 'Queen of Hindsight' on several occasions, airing her grievances about the task whenever the team lost a challenge. However, as a team leader, Lucinda actually excelled in tasks. She listened to others, gave instructions clearly, and assigned tasks calmly and effectively. Because she was in control, she felt more comfortable with engaging in the task, and she succeeded in steering her team to victory. So, although she might have been a better leader than follower, it is still important for each team player to be willing to adapt their role in any given task. As Sugar has learned from his own personal experience, there is no use in being a 'one-trick pony' when it comes to working with other people. Sugar might be a born leader, but he also works as part of a team. Striking the right balance between leader and follower can be very difficult, but Sugar is proof that if you get it right, it can reap huge benefits.

> **There is nothing wrong with voicing concerns as long as these opinions are constructive.**

A positive attitude is a key ingredient to successful teams. If one team member has a drop in standards, then it really impacts on the rest of the team. Kate Walsh from Series 5 shone through as a real contender during all of the tasks, up until Week 7. The task was to find products to sell to major retailers. Uncharacteristically, Kate and two of her team-mates, Ben and Phil, failed to take the task seriously and ended up selling nothing at all.

'Golden girl' Kate ended up in the boardroom trying to defend her position, which she admittedly did with her usual grace and professionalism. But there is no doubt that after her lacklustre performance on the task, her team-mates saw her in a new light and suddenly she was no longer the only real contender in the competition. Consistency of character is so important when working within a team; if you let your standards drop or display uncharacteristic behaviour, then that promotes a sense of unease and distrust among the group.

BE SELF-AWARE

It can be tricky to handpick the perfect dream team, where everybody gets on well and works to the optimum level. You don't have to have a great relationship with each team-mate to succeed, but there must be a high degree of respect for the skills each individual is able to display. Debra Barr from Series 5 of *The Apprentice* might have been known for her 'bulldozing' manner, and lack of diplomacy, but she was respected among her fellow competitors for her keen eye and excellent sales technique. Indeed, Barr was actually quite popular with her team-mates, who although disliking her demanding attitude, respected her leadership skills and her ability to make a sale. Although Barr had a lot to learn in the way she communicated to people, it was clear that she was bright and driven, and would be a success in the future.

So, it is clear that a contestant like Barr needed to work on her personal self-awareness in order to realize the effect her behaviour had on others. This is, perhaps, the most important lesson she learned from her experience on *The Apprentice*. Paul Torrisi had a similar wake-up call in Series 1. Torrisi's legendary temper was extremely entertaining for *Apprentice* viewers but took its toll on his team-mates. When Torrisi was eventually fired, he seemed genuinely hurt by all the negative feedback he had received from his team-mates and Sugar himself. He stated that before he had entered the competition nobody had ever said a bad word about him. Sugar told him to go away and figure out why he had been the object of so much hostility. Like Barr, Torrisi learned a valuable lesson from his time on *The Apprentice*: to treat people with respect and learn to control his temper!

Losing control is a sure-fire way to alienate people and damage professional relationships. In Torrisi's case, even when he excelled in a task, his team-mates insisted on bringing him back into the boardroom time and again. Baffled by what he saw as the injustice of the team's behaviour, Torrisi only became more and more incensed and failed to exercise self-control even in front of Sugar. It was this behaviour that prompted Sugar to send him packing in the end.

However, although Torrisi's temperament wasn't exactly suitable for a team environment, when he did lose control, there was an element of humour in his ranting, rather than spite. Despite his fiery attitude, Torrisi was still likeable enough to get away with some of his more offensive comments.

However, Jenny Celerier from Series 4 lacked the 'likeability' factor; her acerbic comments reduced her team-mate Lucinda Ledgerwood to tears. Celerier seemed to constantly shoot down the ideas of others in a flash and made sure she blamed everybody else for her mistakes. She fiercely fought her corner in the boardroom and played the boardroom 'blame-game' to a tee. Following the bargaining task in Morocco, Celerier was finally given her marching orders by Sugar following an attempt to bribe a market trader not to sell to the other team. These dirty tactics, together with her 'take-no-prisoners' attitude didn't win any favours with Sugar and in the first double-firing of the series, Celerier and fellow contestant Jenny Maguire were sent out of the competition.

> **Losing control is a sure-fire way to alienate people and damage professional relationships.**

Bringing down your team-mates and pointing out their weaknesses in a way that ends up humiliating an individual is a form of bullying, and will not be tolerated in the workplace. Ann, an IT project manager for a hedge fund, remembers how one of her team-mates was so critical of her that it almost destroyed her confidence:

> 'He would constantly point out my personal "weaknesses" in front of others, and tell me that I needed to be stronger if I was going to play with the "big boys". Every time I set a new goal, he would question me to such an extent that I began to start doubting and second-guessing myself. Suddenly, I didn't feel like the project manager any more, and he started to take over the team meetings. Nobody else on the team appreciated his patronizing, critical attitude, but everybody seemed to be too afraid to stand up to him. Morale in the team was low and suddenly we all lacked motivation. Mistakes were made, goals were not reached and it became clear that we weren't working well. Eventually, I found the courage to talk to my boss about the situation and the individual in question was assigned to another task. The relief was almost palpable when he left, and the team was soon back on track, but it shocked us all that one person could have such a negative effect on the group.'

So, as Sugar constantly reiterates, there is no space for egos in a team environment; if the team does not work and support each other, then the whole task is sure to be a complete and utter disaster.

MAKE 'EM LAUGH

As the comedian Robert Orben once said, 'If you can laugh together, you can work together'.

Although working as a team requires intense concentration and hard work, there is nothing wrong with a bit of light relief. Indeed, taking time out to bond with each other in a social environment can be an important way for everybody to get to know each other and provide cohesion in the team. The rewards given to the winning *Apprentice* teams help the members to unwind from all the stress and pressure of the tasks, and help them to get to know each other in a more relaxed environment, which helps them to bond a bit more. Although the apprentices are highly competitive, they are still able to form close bonds and friendships that help them to support each other through the gruelling weeks.

If the team does not work and support each other, then the whole task is sure to be a complete and utter disaster.

The tasks in *The Apprentice* are usually quite intense, and sometimes a bit of humour can do wonders to lift the mood of the contestants – and even Sugar himself. Simon Ambrose, eventual winner of Series 3 of *The Apprentice*, provided one of the best TV comedy moments during the 'home shopping' task. Each of the teams had to choose products to sell on a home shopping channel; the team that sold the most and earned the most money won the task. As leader, Ambrose was a bit of a maverick and chose a wheelchair as one of his products, against the better judgement of the rest of his team-mates. A wheelchair is very specifically tailored to the individual and, generally, not a product that would encourage people to buy off a home shopping channel. But Ambrose, as enthusiastic as ever, persevered with his idea and included it as one of his products.

However, it was the other product choice of trampoline that caused the real stir. As if bouncing up and down and star-jumping wasn't enough, Ambrose provided the real comedy moment when he decided to demonstrate how easy it was to assemble the trampoline. Unbeknown to Ambrose, screwing and unscrewing each of the legs of the trampoline gave rather the wrong impression. The appearance of a lewd sexual gesture, combined with Ambrose's sheer innocence had the whole nation in stitches. Even Sugar had a chuckle over Ambrose's antics. However, the lack of wheelchair sales meant that Ambrose and his team ended up in the boardroom, and the firing ensued.

Humour, in the right places, can be very useful in pressurized situations when nerves are frayed and patience is lacking.

Humour, in the right places, can be very useful in pressurized situations when nerves are frayed and patience is lacking. Of course, it must be the right type of humour targeted at an audience that will respond well to it. There is nothing to gain by making crass jokes and making comments at other people's expense. In some instances, Sugar uses his sense of humour in the boardroom, which serves to lift the tension and helps to make his apprentices (and the viewing public) a little more relaxed and at ease.

However, although a bit of 'down-time' can be useful to help the team bond together, it must not detract from the main objective. Setting goals is a crucial part of teamwork, but this is also a stage where many teams go wrong. Initial team meetings are all about what needs to be done, who is going to carry out each task, and the results that need to be achieved. However, some teams are more about the talk than the action, and they end up missing out on achieving their original goal. It is a well-known fact that we are unable to focus or concentrate for any more than an hour at a time, so two- or three-hour meetings can never be totally productive.

Many of *The Apprentice* teams have fallen foul of the 'talkative' approach by spending far too long hashing out the details of the task, thus wasting time and being unable to deliver at the end.

These days, 'meeting-itis' is prolific among bigger organizations, where employees spend most of the day in meetings talking about goals but don't do anything to make them happen. It is not enough just to discuss what needs to be done; in fact, when we are in meetings, there is no action being taken at all – nothing is getting done. As one frustrated analyst says:

> 'All I do is go from one meeting to the other. By the end of each one, I have so many action points that my head starts to spin. As all my day is taken up with discussions which I feel, quite frankly, are only ways to waste time and allow people to enjoy the sound of their own voices, I have very little time to actually carry out the tasks I have been assigned. Therefore, I end up working late and through the weekends just to catch up, but even then, I feel like I'm chasing my tail most of the time.'

One of Sugar's pet hates is meetings that take longer than they should. In his world, products have a very short life-span and getting them to the shelves before competitors is the difference between success and failure. Some teams become so embroiled in their strategy-setting that they forget about the market and by the time they finally reach a decision, the world has moved on and they have missed the boat. Sugar always makes sure that his team meetings are short, clear and to the point. A man of few words, he is more about action and becomes frustrated with those that do not act quickly enough.

WIN AS A TEAM

Although Sugar is known as bit of a maverick, he is also a team player and it is his ability to nurture strong teams that helps him to consistently deliver his goals. Sugar expects his teams to work hard, respect each other and take pride in meeting their objectives. He also expects the same in his *Apprentice* teams, but sometimes, through jealousy and rivalry, they fall short of his expectations.

- **Work as a team.** The team must be involved at every stage of the process. Sugar believes that clear, concise communication is key when setting goals, and every briefing must end with everybody involved understanding exactly what needs to be done, and the role they must play in achieving the desired result. Withholding information and behaving unpredictably will unsettle the team and cause divisiveness.
- **Cultivate respect and loyalty.** Without respect and loyalty, a team will not succeed. You may not necessarily like your team-mates but you can respect them for their talent, skills, and the ability to get things done.
- **Put aside personal differences.** As *The Apprentice* teams discovered, one of the main challenges of working within a team is getting along with the other team members. A team may be made up of all different sorts of personalities, but there is no room for a personality clash. Team-mates must learn to work together and focus on the goal in order to succeed.

- **Be self-aware.** A lot of the time, we don't realize the affect our behaviour has on other people. People that lack self-awareness tend to make enemies within the team and get defensive if they are offered constructive criticism.
- **Make 'em laugh.** Teamwork does not have to be just about tasks and deadlines, a little light relief can go a long way to bringing people together. Hard work should be rewarded but relaxation must never detract from the main goal.

10

HIRE IN HASTE, REPENT AT LEISURE

'Do not hire a man who does your work for money, but him who does it for love of it.'

– Henry David Thoreau

Creating and maintaining a successful business is dependent on choosing the right people to fit the right roles. Most companies place a great deal of emphasis on the hiring process and take the decision to take on new employees extremely seriously. Putting an unsuitable candidate into a particular role can have enormous financial implications for the company. It is not easy to undo a hasty hiring decision; unsuitable employees cannot simply be fired if they are doing a poor job. Indeed, it can take months and months to legally remove an employee from an organization. With so much at stake, it is little wonder that organizations invest a lot of time and money into perfecting their hiring process.

As a self-starter, Alan Sugar spent his early years working for himself and building up contacts. However, when it came to expanding his business, he had no qualms about taking on people to work for him. Understandably cautious, he tended to employ people he already knew and could trust. However, as time went on and the business really started to take off, he realized that he would have to hire people he didn't necessarily know, and implemented a more formal interviewing process as a result.

Sugar made most of his new hires on the basis of his contacts. He would ask his own employees if they knew a person who would be a suitable candidate for a certain role at Amstrad and then bring them in to give them a good grilling. Sugar also made sure that the potential candidates were thoroughly vetted and, once hired, kept a close eye on them to ensure they were abiding by the Amstrad work ethic.

Although *The Apprentice* interview process or 'the job interview from hell' is far lengthier than Sugar's personal interviewing strategy, it does reflect Sugar's own technique and the standard he expects from his employees. As he believes, 'It is much easier to fire people before you hire them'[1] – meaning that it is better to turn away unsuitable candidates at the interview stage, rather than having the headache of trying to get rid of them when they are a fully-fledged employee. Of course, organizations today do not have the luxury of testing their candidates over a twelve-week period – but with regards to the hiring process, the same lessons very much apply.

USE STRONG-ARM TACTICS

Candidates in *The Apprentice* are put through nothing short of an interview assault course designed to test their selling, buying, designing, marketing, presenting and budgeting skills. As the formidable interviewer, Sugar puts them through their paces, creating tasks to test core business skills. At the end of the interviewing process, he makes a decision based on the candidate's performance during these tasks.

Sugar's technique may seem ruthless but many companies have adopted this type of interviewing style, albeit on a smaller scale. For example, many larger organizations run assessment centres for graduates, where the interviewers monitor the performance of a group of potential candidates over a day or two. This strategy is designed to assess how the group works as a team, determines individual leadership abilities, creativity and motivation.

One interviewer working in a US investment bank describes his role in running assessment centres:

> 'We usually gather together a small group of potential candidates, usually graduates, no more than ten, as we need

to assess each candidate individually. Firstly, we present the group with a "breaking the ice" task, something fun like building a bridge out of paper or making a list of necessities they might need if they find themselves stranded on a desert island. Following this task, the candidates are put through a series of interviews to test their decision-making skills, problem-solving abilities and communication skills.

'Often, we will present a topic to the group to monitor their ability to contribute to a discussion, and judge how they react to being under pressure. After a couple of days, it becomes very obvious who should be put through to the next stage of the interviewing process. The assessment centre technique is, admittedly, demanding for the graduates, but it is also quite exhausting for the interviewers!

'We can't miss a trick when it comes to analyzing the performance of each of the prospective employees and we all have to agree on the best person to put through to the next round. I would say assessment centres are worthwhile but rather vigorous at the same time.'

You could say that Sugar runs his own assessment centre: one that takes place over a number of weeks rather than a couple of days, but the concept is still the same. Perhaps a rigorous interview process is the most sure-fire way to secure the right candidate for the role.

However, there are other ways to test the calibre of future employees. Standard interviews are conducted by one or two people, and there are many corporations that use the same technique as *The Apprentice*, where the interviewees go between rooms to be interviewed by one or more interviewers. A brand manager describes the interviewing process for candidates at her firm:

> *'The prospective employees are interviewed by twelve different people: from the administrative assistant to the head of the department. The interviews might each be conducted by one or two people, and the candidate must go from room to room. The whole process takes place over the course of two days. A discussion follows between the interviewers to decide which candidate is most ideal for the role.'*

The right interviewing technique is crucial for an organization and the interviewer must be comfortable with it. Poor interviewers tend to ask the wrong questions or choose the most unsuitable employees, which can be detrimental for a company.

DON'T GO IT ALONE

Interviewing is rarely an isolated task. Some interviewers may prefer to interview candidates alone, but will usually consult with another party to discuss the suitability of the prospective employee. It is crucial to seek advice from others before taking on a new member of staff; a lone decision could easily end in tears. Alan Sugar has always depended on the advice of others when it comes to the hiring process and never chooses candidates purely on the strength of his own opinions. With regards to *The Apprentice* contestants, although he has come to

Creating and maintaining a successful business is dependent on choosing the right people to fit the right roles.

know them well over a long period, he still relies on Nick and Margaret as well as trusted colleagues to help him make up his mind about who to choose for the job.

To an interviewer, first impressions are important, but in an interview process, it is also vital to look beneath the surface. Just because an interviewee is articulate and well presented does not mean they are the best person for the job. In fact, there are some people out there that are

As the formidable interviewer, Sugar puts them through their paces, creating tasks to test core business skills.

talented at interviews but they might not be the most hardworking when it comes to the job itself. Therefore, it is important not to get carried away with a polished performance but to dig deeper to make sure there is more substance behind the carefully constructed responses. To really make sure you are making the right decision, it is wise to bring the candidate back for a second interview, preferably with someone else in the room.

A senior advertising executive admits how she made a fundamental error by not seeking the advice of her colleagues when hiring a personal assistant:

> 'Usually, two of us do the interviews, but the other person was off sick, so I had no choice but to conduct the interview myself. I thought the candidate was great! Charming, articulate, and it turned out we were from the same village. Of course, we ended up swapping stories about our hometown and people we had in common, etc., and I completely lost track of the formal interviewing structure. By the end of it, I felt we were old pals and I offered the job to her on the spot, which is something I would never normally do.

However, I felt fully confident about my decision, and went ahead with the job offer without consulting anyone else about it.

'Of course, my new PA was a total disaster. I had failed to quiz her on her administrative skills or asked her to provide me with real-life examples from her previous work experience. Over time, I realized that although she had a good personality, she lacked ability and was under the impression that we were "best friends", which undermined my authority somewhat.

'Thankfully, she left of her own accord a couple of months later. When it came to interviewing my next PA, I made absolutely sure that I brought another colleague in with me, and consulted with others about the suitability of the candidate. I definitely learned my lesson!'

So the trick to making the best hiring choices is to always ask the opinions of others before making that crucial decision.

LIST PET PEEVES

As an interviewer, it is important to keep in mind what you absolutely don't want from an interviewee. Making a list of pet peeves does not just involve recording personal preferences, but thinking about the qualities and behaviours that might clash with the company culture. For example, if the working culture is pretty formal and structured, is it wise to hire someone who interviews as scatty and disorganized? Similarly, if the culture is more relaxed, with no major management structure in place, would it be sensible to take on someone who is used to a hierarchical business model?

Alan Sugar has always made himself very clear about his likes and dislikes when it comes to a certain type of person. He knows exactly what he wants from an employee and the rest need not apply. As he says on *The Apprentice*, 'I don't like liars. I don't like cheats. I don't like bullshitters. I don't like schmoozers and I don't like arselickers.'

'I don't like liars. I don't like cheats. I don't like bullshitters. I don't like schmoozers and I don't like arselickers.'

One of Sugar's major pet peeves when it comes to his candidates is lack of preparation. He fully expects the interviewee to have carried out research on the company and be able to talk confidently about what the company does and why they are most suited to the role. Emily Ayre, associate director at top recruitment consultancy Morgan McKinley, agrees that interviewers expect a high degree of preparation from their candidates:

> '"Fail to prepare, prepare to fail" is a true and tested method for interview success. Before any interview, research the prospective employers' product or service offering, what they say about themselves, what others are saying about them, and who their competitors are. You can find most of this information on their website and by using a search engine. Ensure you understand what skills and experience the role requires, and prepare examples and scenarios that highlight your ability to meet the challenges that the new role may offer. The interviewer will have a very clear idea of the perfect candidate and it is how closely you present yourself as a match that will influence their decision.'

It sounds obvious but it is vital that enough research is carried out on the organization before even applying for the job. Interviewers will immediately pick up on lack of preparation and often they will strike poorly prepared interviewees off the list immediately. After all, if the candidates can't be bothered to do a bit of research on the company they supposedly want to work for, then how motivated would they be in the actual role itself?

Most companies will hire someone who is market-savvy (Alan Sugar included), and will expect the interviewees to know about current market trends and the company's competitors. Armed with this sort of information, the interviewers cannot help but be impressed. However, some of the final contestants on *The Apprentice* fell short on their preparation, and frustrated their interviewers beyond belief.

Paul Tulip from Series 2 slipped up in his interviews by trying to bluff his way through them, trying to convince the interviewers that he knew more about Sugar's company than he actually did. It turned out that he knew next to nothing about the firm, its products or what it sold. He also admitted that he lies and cheats every day – not a quality that an interviewer looks for in a potential employee. Although Tulip had excelled in tasks over the weeks and proved himself to be a good salesman with a flair for relating to people, he shot himself in the foot with his dreadful interviewing style and was subsequently eliminated from the final.

It sounds obvious but it is vital that enough research is carried out on the organization before even applying for the job.

Typos or putting down the wrong information are also a source of frustration for interviewers. Badly spelled and inaccurate CVs show an inexcusable lack of preparation. Lee McQueen's CV was full of typing errors, and had even misspelt 'tomorrow', which irritated his formidable interviewer, Claude Littner, beyond belief. Lorraine Tighe from Series 5, who claimed she had a 'sixth sense' for business and finely tuned business instincts, was also caught out during the interview process for having dates wrong on her CV. It turned out that she had overstated her previous term of employment by twelve months. Sheepishly, she explained that she had made a typing error.

Interviewers appreciate an eye for detail and will not tolerate job applications that are messy, incoherent and full of errors.

SPOT THE LIARS!

Interviews can bring out the best or the worst in people. One of the most important parts of being a good interviewer is the ability to read people and make sure that the information provided on CVs is not a work of fiction. It is surprising how many people embellish or lie outright on their CVs, and even worse, think it is acceptable to do so. Thanks to his natural instincts and first-rate ability to read body language, Alan Sugar seems to have an in-built 'liar detector', and looks dimly on insincere and disingenuous people.

Unfortunately, not everybody has Sugar's gift; an IT programmer had the misfortune to interview a person who claimed he had worked in IT for years, and had first-hand knowledge of every software program in existence:

'I had been looking for a decent programmer for a few months, but couldn't find anyone with the right experience. When this guy's CV landed on my desk, I couldn't believe it. It looked like he had exactly the right skills for the role, so I set up an interview with him straight away. At first, the interview went well and he answered the basic questions clearly and accurately. However, as I started to probe his knowledge a little further, he became nervous and started babbling that he knew the answers but his mind had "gone blank".

'I'm no expert in body language, but I could tell by his furious blushing and trembling hands that he was way out of his comfort zone. After the interview, I had my HR department do some background checks; it turned out the company he claimed to have worked for didn't exist and he hadn't even attended the university he had put down on his CV. What's the point of lying on your CV? It's a waste of everybody's time.'

Because Sugar is such an advocate of honesty and straightforwardness, it is still surprising that many of *The Apprentice* candidates exaggerate or straight out lie on their CV, especially when they know they are going to be on national television and the chances of getting away with it are pretty slim.

Lee McQueen provided one of the most hard-to-watch moments in *The Apprentice* so far when he was caught out in a major lie. Uncomfortable with his lack of university education, he wrote on his CV that he had spent two years at university when he had, in reality, only been there for four months. His dishonesty almost cost him the competition, but in the end, Sugar gave him the benefit of the doubt and eventually crowned him as his next apprentice. However, it is never, ever wise to lie on a CV. Most companies do background checks on education and previous roles, and the lies rarely stay hidden.

Again, Emily Ayre from Morgan McKinley agrees: 'While Lee McQueen may have been given the benefit of the doubt, off-screen this finale would have been completely different as often there are several layers of reference checks by recruitment agencies, employers and external referencing agencies, and prospective employers tend not to look kindly on fabricated or exaggerated details on a CV.'

The only reason Lee McQueen escaped a firing was because he had proved himself to an honest and passionate worker over the previous ten weeks. No other employer is going to get to know the candidate in this way or give them the benefit of the doubt if they lie on their CV; being truthful is more appealing to an interviewer. Interviewers prefer people that are upfront about their educational or career blips, and like candidates to be honest about their past mistakes.

THE CIRCLE OF TRUST

'Skilful interviewers know exactly what they want to discover. They have taken exhaustive steps to learn the strategies that will help them employ only the best for their company. They follow a set format for the interview process to ensure objectivity in selection and a set sequence of questions to ensure the facts are gathered. They will definitely test your mettle.' [2]

Martin John Yate

Every boss or head of an organization must be able to trust his business colleagues to interview effectively and deliver the company ethos to the candidates. As a representative of the organization, the interviewer needs to fully understand the company culture and be aware of the type of person they are looking to fill the role.

Therefore, there is a lot of responsibility on the interviewer to ask the right questions, analyze responses (and probe a little deeper if necessary), assess past performance, and determine future potential.

Alan Sugar has handpicked his interviewers to really get the measure of the final few candidates. Most are entrepreneurs that have started their careers young and have risen up the ladder with breathtaking speed. Although the interviewers change from time to time, the most infamous of them all is Claude Littner, Sugar's former global trouble-shooter, who is probably the most terrifying of all the interviewers. His style is very formal and he almost behaves like a headmaster – strict, to the point and not standing for any nonsense. Littner's approach is to find out who can remain calm under enormous pressure and who will crack. Karren Brady, the former managing director of Birmingham City Football Club, takes the opposite approach: she is deceptively nice and has the ability to lull the candidate into a fall sense of security, to the point where they might say too much. Her style is very much centred on getting to know more about the person behind the interview façade, and it is an approach that many interviewers adopt these days.

Sugar's chosen interviewers are familiar with his style and company culture, and know exactly the type of employee he wants to work for him. They also know that Sugar can't stand false pretence or attempts to get the interviewer onside by playing games. The circle of trust is based on this knowledge and Sugar relies on his interviewers to get the real measure of the finalists as they are put through their paces.

Twenty-four-year-old Alex Wotherspoon from Series 4 made the mistake of playing the 'age card' in the boardroom and during the interview process. He made a point of using his age, 'I'm only 24' to account for his lack of work experience and as an excuse for any mistakes he made. Realistically, Wotherspoon should have known that this would not win sympathy from Alan Sugar, a man who left school at 16 and was running a successful business by the age of 21. *The Apprentice* interviewers were similarly unimpressed. When Wotherspoon explained that his CV was so short because he was 'only 24', he had really picked the wrong audience. Karren Brady had been made managing director of Birmingham City Football Club at the age of 23; another interviewer told him in no uncertain terms that he, himself, had been running his own business before the age of 24. Wotherspoon did not gain any ground with the interviewers who were unimpressed with his excuses.

Interviews appreciate an eye for detail and will not tolerate job applications that are messy, incoherent and full of errors.

Interviewers must always be thorough, whether they are quizzing the candidates effectively and efficiently, or making sure background checks are being carried out. Most employers expect their interviewees to provide the names of a couple of referees, if not on the CV, then at a later date when the candidate is going through the last stages of the interviewing process. Referees are generally people that the candidate has worked with in the past (preferably those with seniority) and will vouch for their ability to do a good job, solve problems, get on with others or explain how they made a positive difference in your previous role.

Of course, every interviewer expects a glowing report from each referee that has been provided on the CV, but sometimes this is not the case. The forceful Debra Barr from Series 5 of *The Apprentice* cemented her downfall when she failed to obtain approval from her referees before she included their details on her CV. Despite Debra's assertions that she had got on well with everybody in her previous job, it transpired that her previous employers thought otherwise. The message was clear: Debra did a good job and always delivered, but it was, usually, at the expense of her work colleagues. The negative references and comments about her aggressive attitude and general poor conduct in the workplace proved to be her undoing in the boardroom – and Sugar, albeit reluctantly, sent her packing.

'What's the point of lying on your CV? It's a waste of everybody's time.'

Alan Sugar's interviewers are all tough in their different ways but they do present a realistic picture of what an interview can be like. Interviewing styles very much depend on the individual's personality, which is what makes them unpredictable. Restaurant owner (and eventual winner of Series 5) Yasmina Siadatan was visibly taken aback when she was questioned about the business figures from her restaurant. Instead of taking a few moments to let the question sink in, she shot back defensively, demanding that the interviewer, Claude Littner, tell her how he had obtained the figures. Although a keen businesswoman, she didn't appear to realize that because her restaurant was registered as a limited company, anybody could access the data. Flustered, she became confused about the difference between gross and net profit, and even struggled with providing the correct turnover figures from the restaurant. Yasmina never really recovered in that interview and it clearly left her shaken and subdued. However, she excelled in the other interviews, which were enough to secure her a place in the final and eventually the title of apprentice.

An interview requires the candidates to sell themselves. This is exactly what Sugar is looking for in his next apprentice: the ability to be confident and to know their own skills, strengths and weaknesses. However, there is a difference between being confident and being a bit over the top.

Natural entertainer and funnyman James McQuillan made some pretty unusual assertions on his *Apprentice* application form. In a rather unbusinesslike manner, he claimed that he 'brings ignorance to the table'. Although statements like this serve to grab the attention of any interviewer, they are unprofessional and should definitely be avoided. Predictably, McQuillan was dragged over hot coals during the interview process for his crude approach and for the first time in the series, the funnyman lost his sense of humour and became quite nervous and defensive.

Similarly, Lee McQueen had included in his application form that one of his skills was his 'reverse pterodactyl' impression. Needless to say, the impression left the interviewers cold, and it wasn't something that scored him any brownie points.

Conversely, Kate Walsh from Series 5 remained calm, collected and the model of a professional businesswoman throughout the twelve weeks of *The Apprentice*. She is probably the only contestant to date that has not had a fit of temper or lost her head during one of the tasks. Consistently pitch-perfect, her presentation skills were impeccable; she delivered on every task; she was a good team leader and came across as an all-round skilled businesswoman. However, despite her obvious talents, Kate didn't win. Her measured and calm approach left Sugar and his interviewers thinking that she was 'robotic' and that she lacked personality. During the interview process, she answered every single question perfectly, but gave nothing of herself away. Interviewers like to see passion and enthusiasm from candidates, and a little emotion (but not too much!) can go a long way to convince the interviewer of your desire to work for them.

HIRE IN HASTE, REPENT AT LEISURE

Hiring mistakes can prove costly and inconvenient to an organization. It is not easy just to dispense of badly performing employees, so it is best to make the right hiring choices at the very beginning. Alan Sugar has always been very thorough when it comes to hiring new employees, and has adopted an interviewing technique that really works. The interviewing tactics he employs may be tough, but they always succeed in helping him choose the best person for the job.

- **Use strong-arm tactics.** Most organizations have their own style of interviewing, but irrespective of the models they use, the process must be thorough and challenging. Sugar's tactics are demanding but bring out the best (and worst) in people.
- **Don't go it alone.** It is a huge decision to hire a new employee and big decisions are rarely made by just one person. Throughout his career, Sugar has always consulted others on the validity of candidates, and actively seeks advice from his trusted colleagues on *The Apprentice*.

- **List pet peeves.** As an interviewer it is important to understand what you don't want in an employee to determine if they are the best fit for your organization. Sugar is very prescriptive about his pet peeves and refuses to hire anybody who falls into a certain category.
- **Spot the liars.** With a talent for weeding out the liars, and those that operate under false pretences, Sugar has rarely been hoodwinked into making a poor hiring decision.
- **The circle of trust.** Higher management must trust that the interviewer is asking the right questions and making the right decisions. Sugar has built his own circle of trust and his interviewers follow his hiring model to the letter.

HOW TO NEGOTIATE
THE ALAN SUGAR WAY

Business mogul, tough negotiator or media star? Whatever role he takes on, Alan Sugar makes a success of it. As a revolutionary during his Amstrad days, he created a business model that was truly unique. His distinctive presenting style on *The Apprentice* has won him a whole host of fans and admirers across a wide demographic. Behind the blunt manner lies a sharp intellect, a keen sense of humour, a natural gift for negotiation, and an uncanny instinct for the next big thing. He may be difficult to emulate, but his approach to business is deceptively simple, practical and straightforward.

For those who would like to follow in his footsteps, the following summarizes the ten secrets of his success.

1   DON'T PUSH OR SHOVE

Alan Sugar may be famous for his gruff manner and no-nonsense attitude, but he is no bully. His assertiveness and honesty has won him many a business deal, and the admiration of millions of people, inside and outside the business world.

- Speak your mind
- Have a twinkle in your eye
- Assertiveness rules
- Give bullies short shrift
- Don't be a fuddy-duddy

2   START A REVOLUTION

With his uncanny instinct for spotting a market trend and keen eye for detail, Sugar managed to crash through class barriers with his low-cost, value for money products and no-nonsense advertising.

Being innovative requires a creative mind but also an ability to take calculated risks. The 1980s were truly a golden era for Amstrad, which was fast becoming a force to be reckoned with.

- Do your homework
- Innovation is everything
- Know your market
- Revolutionize your world
- Always look for the next big thing

3   KNOW YOUR CUSTOMER

With his tough but honest approach, coupled with absolute deter-mination and total self-belief, Sugar has proved himself to be the ultimate salesman. Before he even entered his teens, the young Alan Sugar demonstrated a unique talent for sales. Not only did he have a natural instinct for business, but he was able to read peo-ple, and ascertain exactly what they wanted. It was these qualities that helped Sugar become one of the country's most successful entrepreneurs.

- Read your customer
- Trust your instincts
- Get your hands dirty
- Go one step further
- Personality counts

4   STAY TRUE TO YOUR VALUES

From a young age, Sugar understood the importance of applying a core set of business values that he based on his own personal beliefs. Setting business principles is not just a corporate strategy, but involves an emotional as well as a practical investment. The success of a company very much depends on its leader and the example they set to their employees and others that they come into contact with. Through the support of his family, Sugar was able to build up a good company culture with an excellent reputation and develop an enterprise that was known for its integrity and reliability.

- Make good on promises
- Be good to your staff
- Give something back
- Choose family over profit
- Stay true to yourself

5   LEARN FROM YOUR MISTAKES

Throughout his extensive career, Alan Sugar has made some good and not-so-good decisions. However, his total belief in learning from his mistakes has allowed him to recover from his various falls from grace, earning the respect from both his peers and the public. Today, Sugar's star is on the rise and his popularity, which transcends generations, knows no bounds.

- Don't fall at the first hurdle
- Keep your eye on the ball
- Saddle up and ride out the storm
- Backing the wrong horse
- Shun sugar-coating

6   DRIVE A HARD BARGAIN

He may have a reputation for being a tough negotiator and he is certainly competitive, but it is his negotiating style that has earned Alan Sugar the respect of his many business associates. Straight-talking and to the point, Sugar doesn't mess around when there is a good deal on the table, but he also listens to the views of others and treats people fairly and with respect. He is a quick decision-maker and always comes through on his promises – qualities that have been essential in maintaining long-term business relationships.

- Reach for the stars
- Use your network
- Patience is a virtue
- Nurture relationships
- Wrap it up

7   INVEST IN THE RIGHT PEOPLE

The importance of people in relation to the success of an organization can never be underestimated. Investing in the right sort of staff is a skill in itself and takes time, intuition and careful consideration. Choosing the wrong employee can have serious ramifications for an organization and can prove to be a costly mistake. Sugar chooses his apprentices based not only on his gut instinct but through their ability to prove themselves as being worthy contenders for the six-figure salary. Week after week, he weeds out the pretenders, the charmers, the motormouths and the manipulators, until he arrives at his final decision in week 12. For the most part, his apprentices have proved to be assets to his various companies and have remained loyal to their boss.

- Surround yourself with loyal staff
- Beware of the pretenders
- Stay clear of the temper tantrums
- Trust your intuition
- Don't hire people exactly like yourself

8   LEAD FROM THE FRONT

Alan Sugar is a born leader who has the inbuilt talent and qualities to inspire and motivate others. He is tough but fair, and believes in giving praise when it is due. His leadership style is inclusive; he does not create class boundaries or dismiss those who operate in 'lower' level roles. A good listener and speaker, Sugar treats his employees with respect, and they have remained loyal and committed to their leader as a result.

- Lead and nurture
- Engage with your staff
- Lead by example
- Leading a horse to water
- The truth always wins

9   WIN AS A TEAM

Although Sugar is known as bit of a maverick, he is also a team player and it is his ability to nurture strong teams that helps him to consistently deliver his goals. Sugar expects his teams to work hard, respect each other and take pride in meeting their objectives. He also expects the same in his *Apprentice* teams, but sometimes, through jealousy and rivalry, they fall short of his expectations.

- Work as a team
- Cultivate respect and loyalty
- Put aside personal differences
- Be self-aware
- Make 'em laugh

10   HIRE IN HASTE, REPENT AT LEISURE

Hiring mistakes can prove costly and inconvenient to an organiza-tion. It is not easy just to dispense of badly performing employees, so it is best to make the right hiring choices at the very beginning. Alan Sugar has always been very thorough when it comes to hiring new employees, and has adopted an interviewing technique that really works. The interviewing tactics he employs may be tough, but they always succeed in helping him choose the best person for the job.

- Use strong-arm tactics
- Don't go it alone
- List pet peeves
- Spot the liars
- The circle of trust

THE LAST WORD

There are many words that have been used to describe the inimitable Alan Sugar – admittedly, not all of them totally flattering. Belligerent, gruff, blunt, bossy, stubborn, demanding, difficult to impress … although he hasn't made it to where he is today by being Mr Nice Guy, behind the tough exterior is a family man who abides by a firm set of personal values. Undoubtedly, he has high standards and elevated expectations when it comes to business, but it is his uncompromising approach and expert negotiating skills that have won him a great deal of admiration and respect from his peers.

As a young man, he rolled up his sleeves and stood up to the City sceptics who held a dim view of this scruffy boy from east London. Shocked at first by Sugar's brusque business style, the top financiers soon realized that this was no amateur they were dealing with. This was a man who operated with breathtaking speed; was fast and furious when making decisions; and negotiated like a pro. Over time, Sugar gained a reputation as a formidable negotiator, one that still applies today.

Perhaps the real secret to Sugar's success is that he has always stayed true to himself. Come hell or high water, Sugar has refused to change his behaviour or adjust the way he does things, irrespective of the criticism he receives. At one time or another, Sugar has been at the brunt of several media onslaughts, firstly as an unconventional young entrepreneur who had the cheek to take on the big boys (or so he was portrayed); followed by his decade of unpopularity as chairman of Tottenham Hotspur; and finally, the recent flak he has received for his government peerage and 'enterprise czar' role. In spite of the negative comments from the media, Sugar always takes the higher ground, and stays exactly as he is: feisty, generous, humorous, brutally honest and sharp as a tack.

The last 40 years have been an enlightening time for Alan Sugar. He fought his way out of poverty, learned the tricks of the trade, built a multi-million pound company out of nothing but his own business talent, tough negotiating skills and pure common sense, and created a unique business model that revolutionized both society and the face of business forever. It is impossible to pigeon-hole a man that wears so many hats, and has achieved so much. Let's just say that he is a role model for every struggling entrepreneur that dreams of making it big – perhaps this is the hat that suits him the best.

NOTES

THE LIFE AND TIMES OF ALAN SUGAR

1   Thomas, David, 'What you see is what you get', *The Daily Telegraph*, 16 February, 2005.
2   Sugar, Sir Alan, *The Apprentice: How To Get Hired Not Fired*, BBC Books, 2005, p.182.

CHAPTER ONE

1   Teeman, Tim, 'Sir Alan Sugar: talking tough', *The Times*, 26 March, 2008.
2   Gwyther, Matthews & Saunders, Andrew, 'The MT 40 Interview: Sir John Harvey-Jones', *Management Today*, 1 September, 2006.
3   Robertson, Colin, 'Sir Alan Sugar: I'm not a bully', *The Sun*, 26 March, 2008.
4   Burden, Charlie, *Sir Alan Sugar: The Biography*, John Blake, London, 2009, p. 190.
5   Jeffries, Mark, 'Apprentice star Sir Alan Sugar on why there's more to life than money', *Daily Mirror*, 26 March, 2008.

CHAPTER TWO

1   Sugar, Sir Alan, *The Apprentice: How To Get Hired Not Fired*, BBC Books, 2005, p. 122.
2   Thomas, David, *The Amstrad Story*, Century, London, 1990, p. 56–7.
3   Burden, Charlie, *Sir Alan Sugar: The Biography*, John Blake, London, 2009, p. 49.
4   Rohrer, Finlo, 'Nostalgia for a techno cul-de-sac', BBC News Online, 1 August, 2007.
5   Thomas, David, *The Amstrad Story*, Century, London, 1990, p. 181.

CHAPTER THREE

1   Treneman, Ann, 'Apprentice in the Lords: Baron Sugar of Clapton takes his seat', *The Times*, 21 July, 2009.
2   Thomas, David, *The Amstrad Story*, Century, London, 1990, p. 53.

CHAPTER FOUR

1   Sugar, Sir Alan, *The Apprentice: How To Get Hired Not Fired*, BBC Books, 2005, p. 81.
2   Ibid.
3   Burden, Charlie, *Sir Alan Sugar: The Biography*, John Blake, London, 2009, p. xxv.
4   Morgan, Piers, 'How Sir Alan Sugar celebrated his 40th wedding anniversary with a £2m party', *Daily Mail*, 14 May, 2009.

CHAPTER FIVE

1   Austin, Simon, 'Sugar leaves sour taste', BBC Sport Online, 21 December, 2000.
2   Burden, Charlie, *Sir Alan Sugar: The Biography*, John Blake, London, 2009, p. 97.
3   *The Real Sir Alan Sugar*, BBC, 11 January, 2009.
4   *Ibid*.
5   Appleyard, Brian, 'Alan Sugar and *The Apprentice*', *The Sunday Times*, 6 February, 2005.

CHAPTER SIX

1   Burden, Charlie, *Sir Alan Sugar: The Biography*, John Blake, London, 2009, p. 77.

2   Kennedy, Gavin, *Negotiation: An A–Z Guide*, Economist Books, 2009, p. 5.

CHAPTER SEVEN

1   Sugar, Sir Alan, *The Apprentice: How To Get Hired Not Fired*, BBC Books, 2005, p. 117.
2   Thapar, Neil, 'Sugar heading towards bitter exit from City: The Amstrad boss has tired of life in the public glare', *The Independent*, 27 September 1992.

CHAPTER EIGHT

1   Adair, John, *Not Bosses but Leaders: How to Lead the Way to Success*, Kogan Page, London, 2002, p. 130.
2   Thomas, David, *The Amstrad Story*, Century, London, 1990, p. 256.

CHAPTER NINE

1   Sugar, Sir Alan, *The Apprentice: How To Get Hired Not Fired*, BBC Books, 2005, p. 30.
2   Lencioni, Patrick, *The Five Dysfunctions of a Team: A Leadership Fable*, Jossey Bass, 2002.

CHAPTER TEN

1   Sugar, Sir Alan, *The Apprentice: How To Get Hired Not Fired*, BBC Books, 2005, p. 207.
2   Yate, Martin John, *Great Answers to Tough Interview Questions*, 6th edition, Kogan Page, London, 2005, p. 145.

INDEX

EMMA MURRAY

Emma Murray is a freelance writer and ghostwriter, with a background in investment banking. She specializes in non-fiction, primarily business, psychology, history and memoir. She is also the author of many articles on freelancing, which have appeared in various trade publications, including *The Author* magazine. She lives in London with her husband, Sam.
(www.emmamurray.net)